Pra

What are som
leaders already praying for pastors?

Father, bless your servants, the pastors of your churches. May they continually sense your presence. May each of them feel your proximity as they minister to your people and accomplish your will daily. May they know that their work is entirely in your hands as they love your children, both the committed and the uncommitted.

—TOM PHILLIPS, Executive Director, Billy Graham Library

Lord Jesus, I pray for pastors today who are struggling with discouraging circumstances in their own lives. May they, as the psalmist says, find their strength in you and continue to set their hearts on pilgrimage. Make for them springs in their desert place (see Psalm 84:5–7).

—GEORGE O. WOOD, General Superintendent,
The General Council of the Assemblies of God

Sovereign God, you hold every pastor in your hands. You are his security, his helper, and his hope. Whatever his needs, meet them. Whatever his weaknesses, protect him. Whatever his strengths, restrain him. Whatever his future, release him. I pray in Jesus' name that you will protect him from himself, ignite him by the power of the Spirit, and renew him to believe again … that he can change the world. In Jesus' name, amen.

—RONNIE FLOYD, Senior Pastor, Cross Church,
Former President of the Southern Baptist Convention

Lord Jesus, fill the harvesters in the field with a zealous, overflowing love for you. May you daily renew in them a love for your people and those who might come to know you. Fill them with your Spirit—to speak as you would speak, to serve as you would serve, and to love as you have first loved us. Heavenly Father, give your servants joy in the work that you have prepared for them to do, bestowing riches that only you can give, blessing them with peace that only you can bring.

—Samuel Rodriguez, President, National Hispanic
Christian Leadership Conference

Our loving Father, please enable your shepherds to tend the flock you have entrusted to them with the love of Jesus. May they love you and your people as you love them. May they also love and share with those outside the flock so they may come to know and follow our Great Shepherd, Jesus Christ!

—Paul Cedar, Chair and CEO,
Mission America Coalition

Father God, thank you that you have called, commissioned, and empowered pastors after your own heart. I pray for their protection, provision, and continued anointing upon their ministries.

—Sam Clements, General Overseer,
Church of God of Prophecy

Heavenly Father, encourage pastors in their divine calling. Quiet their hearts from the busyness of "doing" for you, and allow them to rediscover the wonder of "being" with you. It is here, sitting at your feet, that your shepherds will be empowered by the Holy Spirit with strength for today, hope for tomorrow, and joy for the journey.

—Tim Coalter, North American Presbyter,
Church of God of Prophecy

Father, help our pastors to grow so that our churches will grow, and to be healthy so our churches will be healthy. Help them to walk with you today in such a way that they can finish strong later. Thank you for the privilege to love, lead, and feed your people.

—Mark Dance, Director, Lifeway Pastors

Father, woo pastors from the carousel of busyness into the beauty of your holy presence. Lift them from the grind of schedules to the glory near your heart, where they may embrace anew the joy of romancing and dancing with you. Hurl them into the harvest, where your love will draw the last, the least, and the lost.

—JEFF FARMER, President, Pentecostal/Charismatic
Churches of North America

Abba Father, bless your shepherds as they impart life-change. Transform pastors first, as they walk in the light of your Son, your Word, and your people. May your servants have fresh encounters with Jesus, frequent experiences in the Word, and faithful engagement with your people. Allow them to experience the joy of joining their flocks in a life-changing journey with Jesus. I humbly pray in Jesus' name, amen!

—MICHAEL LEWIS, Senior Pastor, Roswell Street Baptist Church,
Former Pastor of Pastors, North American Mission Board

We offer our sincere prayers for pastors who speak God's Word to us. Empower them to share transformational truths with wisdom, courage, and power. Bless them physically, emotionally, and spiritually.

—ALTON GARRISON, Assistant General Superintendent,
The General Council of the Assemblies of God

Lord, bless today's pastor with a soft, empathetic heart that connects with the brokenness in our generation and a resolve of steel that stands firm in the collapsing morality of our day. Please give him supernatural compassion and courage at the same time.

—WILLIAM M. WILSON, President,
Oral Roberts University

My Heavenly Father, I pray for Pastor _____, that today his faith would be strengthened and his eyes and ears would be open to hear your whispers of encouragement and see the depth of your compassion toward him and his family. I pray he will be seized by overwhelming gratitude for the great support of the Spirit and the undergirding of your angels. Please love on him and his family deeply today!

—RONNIE C. CRUDUP, Sr., Presiding Bishop,
Fellowship of International Churches

Dear Father, as you instructed the disciples to distribute the fish and the loaves, so have you charged pastors today to share your nourishing word. May they remember that you are the source to whom they must constantly return if they are to accomplish your purpose for them.

—CHARLES E. BLAKE, Sr., Presiding Bishop,
Church of God in Christ

Father God, I pray pastors would have anointed and enriching encounters with you as they study your Word. May you lead them to boldly and vulnerably share from their personal life experiences the transforming power of a deepening relationship with you, so that others will long to live Spirit-empowered lives of faith and hope.

—KAY HORNER, Awakening America Alliance
and The Helper Connection

Lord Jesus, Bridegroom of the church, thank you for shepherding your shepherds as they care for your flock. Confirm their sense of calling, sustain their commitment to your truth, fill them with your servant-hearted love for those you've entrusted to their care. Protect them from pride, discouragement, and unwise comparisons. Enable them to be shrewd as serpents and harmless as doves as they minister in an increasingly apathetic, antagonistic culture.

—TODD SORENSON, Vice President, Barna Group
and Men's Ministry Lay Leader

Thank you, Lord, for not only calling pastors, but also for power from you to fill them with hope and strength.

—RANDALL BACH, President, Open Bible Churches

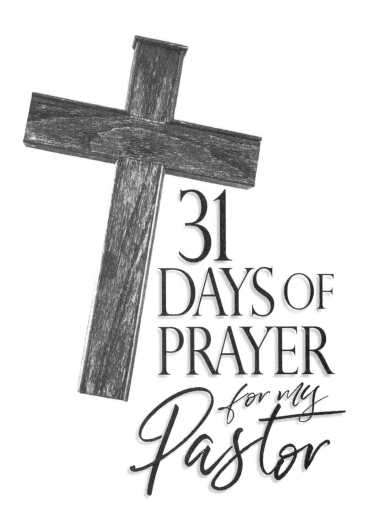

31
DAYS OF
PRAYER
for my
Pastor

BroadStreet
PUBLISHING

BroadStreet Publishing Group, LLC
Racine, Wisconsin, USA
BroadStreetPublishing.com

31 DAYS OF PRAYER *for My Pastor*

Executive editor: Terri Snead

ISBN-13: 978-1-4245-5540-6 (softcover)
ISBN-13: 978-1-4245-5541-3 (e-book)

Stock or custom editions of BroadStreet Publishing titles may be purchased in bulk for educational, business, ministry, fundraising, or sales promotional use. For information, please e-mail info@broadstreetpublishing.com.

Cover design by Chris Garborg at garborgdesign.com
Typesetting by Katherine Lloyd at theDESKonline.com

Printed in the United States of America
17 18 19 20 21 5 4 3 2 1

CONTENTS

A SPIRIT-EMPOWERED DISCIPLE
LOVES THE LORD

A SPIRIT-EMPOWERED DISCIPLE
LIVES THE WORD

A SPIRIT-EMPOWERED DISCIPLE
LOVES PEOPLE

A SPIRIT-EMPOWERED DISCIPLE
LIVES HIS MISSION

INTRODUCTION

*I*t's no surprise that our world is headed in the wrong direction. It often seems that the only thing constant is change: the culture is changing, the people are changing, and there's even a growing skepticism of churches and of Christians. We may not always know what to do in the midst of these changes, but we know the one who is never-changing. We know the one who is the same yesterday, today, and forever (see Hebrews 13:8).

As we look to the Lord for direction, we can also call upon Him to raise up and equip faithful leaders for our day. The world needs confident, committed pastors who will champion the name of Jesus and lift the mantle of God and His people. As Jesus-followers, we need wise, humble, Spirit-empowered leaders to help us navigate the complexities of this world. That's why we invite you to be part of praying for your pastor. We hope this resource facilitates a groundswell of Christ's followers who are committed to praying for God's shepherds.

Day 1

WHY TO PRAY
FOR MY PASTOR

*W*hy should we take the time or make it a priority to pray for our pastors? Setting aside thirty-one days to pray for our shepherds makes sense for many reasons. Here are just a few:

- As we pray for our pastors, we're joining Jesus as He prays on their behalf.

Hebrews tells us that "[Jesus] lives forever to intercede with God on [our] behalf" (Hebrews 7:25). And the book of Romans reminds us that "he is sitting in the place of honor at God's right hand, pleading for us" (Romans 8:34). Don't you imagine the Savior's prayer list includes the names of the pastors who are called to complete His mission? Let's join Jesus in praying for our shepherds.

- As we pray for our pastors, we're joining Jesus in His celebrations.

In Christ's last moments on earth, He revealed His loving desire for us. Jesus prayed that "My joy may be in you, and that your joy may be made full" (John 15:11 NASB). Jesus finds joy in our pastors' surrender to His calling and their life of dedication to Him. So let's join Jesus in celebrating our shepherds.

- As we pray for our pastors, we're joining Jesus in His concern.

The apostle Peter faced challenges in his life, just as our own pastors do. One of the most divinely appointed pastors in history struggled with failure and discouragement. And this was Jesus' response: "But I have prayed for you, that your faith may not fail; and you, when once you have turned again, strengthen your brothers" (Luke 22:32 NASB). Peter's challenges, plus Jesus' prayers, became incredible opportunities for expanded ministry. We can't deny that Pentecost was certainly evidence of expanded ministry, birthed out of challenge and opportunity. So let's join Jesus in praying for our pastors, lifting up concerns and asking the Lord to expand and enhance ministry.

- As we pray for our pastors, we strengthen our walk with Jesus.

Praying for our shepherds will have personal benefit because spending time with our Savior deepens closeness with Him. Praying for pastors will strengthen *their* walk with Jesus too. Just as Moses needed Aaron and Hur's support when he grew weary, so our prayers can lift our pastors, bringing encouragement, vision, and support. Finally, praying for our pastors will strengthen our church's ministry. Not everyone can lead worship or work in the church nursery, but every child of God can pray. So let's pray for our pastors! Let's pray often. Let's pray consistently. Let's pray boldly. Let's pray faithfully!

Take the next few moments and join Jesus in prayer.

» Jesus, when I imagine that I can join you in prayer, my heart feels grateful because _____.

» I want to join you in prayer for my pastor. First, I'm grateful for my pastor because _____. I lift up my pastor to you and pray specifically that you would _____.

Day 2

HOW TO PRAY
FOR MY PASTOR

A world where the prince of darkness seeks to steal, kill, and destroy needs Christ-followers who walk in the light (see John 10:10; 12:35 NASB). For the next thirty-one days, we encourage you to take a journey of walking in the light. During your times of prayer, you will walk in the light of God's Son, God's Word, and God's people (see John 8:12; Matthew 5:14; Psalm 119:105). As you take the journey, you will spend moments in personal prayer, but then you will also pray for your pastor. You'll pray for your pastor to:

- encounter Jesus in fresh, new ways,
- experience Scripture frequently, and
- engage God's people in supportive, practical ways.

Let's have a first encounter with Jesus. As you read these words from the Savior, imagine that He is speaking directly to you. Listen for His compassionate, strong voice. He's thrilled to share these moments with you.

A FRESH ENCOUNTER WITH JESUS

The darkness of this world is all around you, and I don't want you to be overtaken. So I have a plan. I have a plan for your protection, guidance, and strength. If you'll spend time with me, my Word, and my people, darkness doesn't have a chance. As you encounter me, I will protect you because I'm the light of the world. Let my Word guide you and light your way. Let my people encourage you and give you strength. Walking in the light is the best place to be because that means we're walking together (see John 8:12; Matthew 5:14; Psalm 119:105).

» Jesus, when I look at the darkness of this world, I feel especially concerned about _____. Lord, I am grateful for your protection, guidance, and strength, particularly because _____.

» Jesus, give us the desire and longing to spend more time with you, your Word, and your people so that darkness doesn't have a chance in our congregation. I ask specifically for protection concerning _____, for guidance concerning _____, and that you would strengthen us in _____.

As you continue this journey of prayer, remember the goal. Your times of prayer can't be focused on changing your pastor or changing your church. These moments with Jesus, His Word, and His people are designed to first develop Christlikeness within you. The destination of your journey is a person, and His name is Jesus. As you spend time focused on getting to know Christ and experiencing more of His love, as you spend time focused on living out His Word, not just reading or hearing it, you'll become more like Him. This journey will change something—and hopefully it's you!

Finally, as you take this journey of prayer, it will also be important to remember this goal: Pastors typically don't need more knowledge or education. They rarely need to hear more information or rational advice. Instead, pastors need more of their own encounters with Jesus and meaningful times of experiencing Scripture. They also need Jesus-followers who will come alongside them, giving them encouragement, support, and fervent prayer.

Day 3

WHAT TO PRAY
FOR MY PASTOR

*T*his book is designed to foster a Spirit-empowered faith—a
faith that is demonstrable, observable, and only possible with
the empowerment of the Holy Spirit. A framework for this kind of
spiritual growth has been drawn from a cluster analysis of several
Greek and Hebrew words that declare that Christ's followers are to
be equipped for works of ministry or service (see Appendix 2, page
117). Therefore, in *31 Days of Prayer for My Pastor,* you'll find specific sections that are designed around four themes. A Spirit-empowered disciple ...

- **Loves the Lord** (see Acts 13:2 NASB). You will find
  seven days of prayer marked L1–L10.

- **Lives the Word** (see Acts 6:4 NASB). You will find
  seven days of prayer marked W1–W10.

- **Loves people** (see Galatians 5:13 NASB). You will find
  seven days of prayer marked P1–P10.

- **Lives His mission** (see 2 Corinthians 5:18 NASB). You
  will find seven days of prayer marked M1–M10.

The ultimate goal of our faith journey is to relate to the person of Jesus as His Spirit enables Great Commission living empowered by Great Commandment love. Our world needs pastors who are living as Spirit-empowered disciples and making disciples who in turn make disciples. Thus, *31 Days of Prayer for My Pastor* rightly focuses on the powerful simplicity of:

- loving God as your first priority,
- living His Word because there's power and possibility in experiencing Scripture,
- loving people by developing a lifestyle of giving first, and
- living His mission, which means building a lasting legacy.

These four themes of Spirit-empowered discipleship are critical to addressing some of the important research findings on *The State of Pastors*, authored by the Barna Group. The research cited in this resource is drawn from *The State of Pastors: How Today's Faith Leaders Are Navigating Life and Leadership in an Age of Complexity*. Additional information on *The State of Pastors*, along with information on how to purchase, is found in the Appendix 4, page 131.

After three days of prayer focused on why, how, and what to pray for our pastors, you will turn your attention to pray around specific research topics identified by the Barna Group. Each day, you will have the opportunity to focus on specific:

- celebrations and points of strength that the research identifies, and
- concerns and areas of growth for pastors, which can turn into opportunities for the Lord.

An "Experience of Scripture" will also be a part of each daily prayer. We've written this resource to guide you in what it looks like and sounds like to actually do the Word—not just hear it (see James 1:22). Your prayer will be an opportunity to live out or experience God's Word. Let's begin by experiencing a few simple but powerful verses.

AN EXPERIENCE OF SCRIPTURE

Rejoice with those who rejoice …
—Romans 12:15 NASB

The Lord is rejoicing in His call, gifting, and leading of your pastor. Pause for a few moments and rejoice with Jesus over your pastor.

» Jesus, I know you are excited to see how we live out your call to leadership, especially how my pastor _____. I am thrilled with you to see my pastor _____.

» Jesus, I am blessed by your gifts for my pastor. I know you must smile to see my pastor living out the gifts you have given.

Bear one another's burdens, and thereby fulfill the law of Christ.
—Galatians 6:2 NASB

Jesus is burdened any time your pastor experiences the heaviness of carrying the burdens of ministry alone. Pause for a moment and join the Lord in a commitment to bear your pastor's burdens.

» Jesus, I know you must be heavy-hearted when you see all the demands on our lives and families. I, too, am feeling compassion for others in ministry about _____.

» Jesus, let's join together in bearing my pastor's burdens and loving my pastor well.

I searched for a man among them who would build up the wall and stand in the gap before Me …
—Ezekiel 22:30 NASB

It is with great joy that we have developed the prayer moments in this resource, the Spirit-empowered discipleship framework (in collaboration with others), and the Spirit-empowered outcomes that are included in the Appendices of this resource (see pages 121–129). Our greatest desire is to serve pastors by creating a groundswell of faithful followers who deepen their relationship with the Lord and stand in the gap for our ministry leaders.

STRATEGIC WAYS TO USE THIS RESOURCE

• Church-Wide Pastor Prayer Emphasis:

Plan a month-long gift that engages your congregation in focused prayer for your pastor. Pastor appreciation is widely celebrated in the month of October, so it could be the perfect time for a church-wide prayer emphasis. An entire month of daily, focused prayer for your pastor would be a phenomenal gift!

• Launch a Pastor Prayer Team:

Imagine the difference prevailing prayer can make as a team from your church supports your pastor(s) with daily prayer.

A small church, with just seven intercessors, can pray for their pastor one day a week. A larger church might have a team of thirty-one prayer warriors, each praying one day a month.

Utilize *31 Days of Prayer for My Pastor* to launch this ministry and visit greatcommandment.net for other prayer team resources, posters, and promotional materials.

A SPIRIT-
EMPOWERED
DISCIPLE

Loves the Lord

QUALITIES OF A GREAT PASTOR

> Allow our *love for the Lord* to be strengthened, refreshed, and renewed. Empower us to prioritize a close, deeply personal relationship with God. Help us to enjoy more moments of thanksgiving with the Lord.

People in the church and community were asked to describe the top two traits that a pastor needs to be successful. Of those surveyed, 48 percent said that a pastor needs to demonstrate a great love for people, while 33 percent said that a pastor needs to demonstrate a great love for God. What an encouragement this is! The public values the same qualities in a pastor that are described as the Great Commandment (see Matthew 22:37–40). This means that we have the right expectations for our pastors!

However, pastors often struggle to find time to deepen their love for the Lord. In fact, almost half (47 percent) of pastors surveyed indicate they find it very difficult or somewhat difficult to invest in their own spiritual development.

STORIES FROM A PASTOR'S HEART

I had been in ministry for more than twenty years. I was an effective shepherd of our congregation; I loved my people well. I was an effective communicator of God's Word, accurately preaching and teaching the truths of Scripture. At the same time, though, I struggled to prioritize my own spiritual growth. On one particular evening, I had a new kind of encounter with Jesus.

I was studying the story of the ten lepers in Luke 17, when I read Jesus' words, "Were not all ten cleansed? Where are the other nine?" (Luke 17:17 NIV). And that's when the Spirit revealed that this wasn't a Savior who needed to know the location of ten lepers; rather, this was a Savior whose heart was acquainted with sorrow and grief (see Isaiah 53:3). This was *my* Savior who felt sadness and disappointment that only one leper had returned to give thanks.

More personally, the Holy Spirit showed me that I had been like one of those nine. I had saddened the heart of my Savior because I rarely took time to express my gratitude. I wept with Jesus. I shared moments of repentance and compassion for Jesus. It was a personal moment of deep connectedness between Jesus and me.

This personal encounter with Jesus brought change in me. I now begin most mornings alone with the Lord. I imagine myself kneeling beside that one leper, giving thanks to Jesus.

A FRESH ENCOUNTER WITH JESUS

Dear child, I delight in providing for you and caring for you. I can't wait to show you compassion and find joy in giving to you. At the same time, it hurts when I have demonstrated my care for you and you don't remember to say, "Thank you." I long to share more moments of gratitude so that we can celebrate together (see Luke 17:17; Isaiah 30:18).

» Jesus, I don't want to be like the nine lepers who forgot to give you thanks. I know it hurts your heart when I don't express my gratitude. When I imagine you feeling sad and disappointed, I feel _____.

» I want to have more personal encounters with you, so
that my love for you is deepened. I pray specifically that
_____. I also pray my pastor would enjoy _____.

AN EXPERIENCE OF SCRIPTURE

*Yes, I will bless the Lord and not forget the glorious things he
does for me.*

—Psalm 103:2 TLB

» God, I give you thanks for how you have _____. Jesus,
I am so grateful for the glorious way you have _____.

» Help us remember your blessings and give thanks. I specifically pray you would give my pastor _____.

ENGAGING GOD'S PEOPLE

Send your pastor a note, e-mail, or text message. Express
your thanks for how God has ministered to you and others
through your pastor. Gratitude is contagious.

CLAIM HIS PROMISES

*Blessed are those who have learned to acclaim you,
who walk in the light of your presence, Lord.*

—Psalm 89:15 NIV

Love the Lord 1:
A Spirit-empowered disciple loves the Lord by practicing
thanksgiving in all things.

Day 5

PERSONAL, SPIRITUAL DEVELOPMENT

Allow our *love for the Lord* to be strengthened, refreshed, and renewed. Let us enjoy more intimate moments with the Lord in prayer and His Word. Help us carve out more times of solitude with Jesus and add seasons of fasting to our spiritual walk.

*P*astors report that times of personal prayer and reading Scripture are the keys to their spiritual development. Eighty-one percent of pastors consider times of prayer as their deepest connection to God, while 71 percent of them enjoy their devotional moments in the Word as key to their spiritual growth. Isn't it wonderful to celebrate that the majority of our pastors identify these as the key spiritual disciplines for growth?

Unfortunately, a pastor's schedule is full, and the busyness of ministry can leave little room for more. That's undoubtedly why few (13 percent) pastors report that times of silence and solitude are consistent parts of their spiritual growth, and even fewer (3 percent) enjoy regular times of prayer and fasting.

STORIES FROM A PASTOR'S HEART

As a young minister, I loved spending time with Paul. He was both my spiritual mentor and a great cook! I was especially fond of his cheese enchiladas and chicken tacos. One weekend, both of our wives left town for a retreat. Paul and I decided to spend the weekend together since the ladies were away. I walked in the front door, mouthwatering, eyes searching for Paul's-also-famous home-made salsa and chips. Much to my disappointment, my friend announced, "David, I'm so excited! I've sensed the Lord wants us to fast and pray this weekend!"

I was heartbroken about the Mexican food but came to admire my friend even more. What Paul began to show me that weekend was that even though they lived in a small three-bedroom home with five children, he and his wife, Mary Ann, had set aside space in their home for a prayer closet. Prayer and fasting was a priority for Paul.

We did have some Mexican food by the end of my stay, but for most of that weekend we prayed, fasted, listened to the Lord, claimed Scripture, and made intercession. Forty years later, Paul's discipline of solitude, prayer, and fasting still shapes my life.

A FRESH ENCOUNTER WITH JESUS

I long to have quiet moments of conversation with you. I love it when you are still and free of distractions, because those are the times when you can truly feel my love. Remember, I am a God of love. So it's in these quiet moments of time with me that I can be your refuge and strength (see Psalm 46:10; 1 John 4:8).

» God, I ask that you quiet my mind and spirit. Help me to focus on you.

» What distractions are keeping us from being still? Jesus, show us any of the distractions that are keeping us from being still before you. I also pray that my pastor _____.

AN EXPERIENCE OF SCRIPTURE

Be still, and know that I am God.

—Psalm 46:10 NIV

» Jesus, I want to be still so that I can soak in your love. In what new ways do you want me to experience your love today?

» Lord, I ask for more of these quiet moments. Help us prioritize time with you, free from distractions and focused on receiving your love. I specifically pray my pastor would enjoy _____.

ENGAGING GOD'S PEOPLE

Talk to your pastor about ways you could support his focused time with God. You might offer to partner together in a season of fasting. Provide a quiet place for your pastor to get away for solitude and prayer. Offer to help your pastor with the list of "things to do" so that there are fewer distractions.

CLAIM HIS PROMISES

Come near to God and he will come near to you.

—James 4:8 NIV

Love the Lord 6:
A Spirit-empowered disciple loves the Lord through the consistent practice of self-denial, fasting, and solitude rest.

Day 6

SPIRITUAL HEALTH

Allow our *love for the Lord* to be strengthened, refreshed, and renewed. Let us experience the real God through deepened closeness and intimacy with Him.

We can celebrate our pastors' perspectives on spiritual health and relationship with the Lord. Overall, pastors report great satisfaction with their quality of life, and as much as 88 percent of ministry leaders indicate that their spiritual health could be described as good or excellent.

In the midst of this overall satisfaction, we still find a point of prayer. A key point of stress seems to be a pastor's sense of inadequacy. Thirty percent of US adults report experiencing feelings of inadequacy at times or with some frequency, but 57 percent of pastors report experiencing these same feelings. Pastors may not feel adequate, but we know the one who is. Let's call on the great I AM to be with our ministry leaders.

STORIES FROM A PASTOR'S HEART

By everyone's account, Pastor Kevin was a great pastor. He visited church members in the hospital, prayed for loved ones, preached moving sermons, and told the world about Jesus. There was just one problem. Kevin's ministry often left his teenage sons feeling alone. They needed their dad, not a pastor.

The situation was at a boiling point after both boys were expelled for vandalizing school property and smoking pot on campus. Heated words were exchanged, but when the boys were finally calm, they told their dad how they really felt. A moment of insight brought these words from Kevin: "I guess I gravitate toward the places where I feel adequate. I know how to prepare a sermon or visit somebody in the hospital. But I don't always know what to do when it comes to being a dad. I'm so sorry that my fear and attention to other things left you boys feeling alone."

With the help of some trusted ministry leaders, Kevin began to learn what it meant to be a father. He learned what a father does by practicing more of who the Father is!

A FRESH ENCOUNTER WITH JESUS

Remember, there is nothing too hard for me. My power is unlimited. I'll ride across the heavens to help you—just call for my help. And when you need to know how or the load is too heavy, come to me. I'll be right there with you. I'm a gentle teacher and compassionate Savior (see Genesis 18:14; Numbers 11:23; Deuteronomy 33:26; 20:4; Matthew 11:28; Isaiah 30:18).

» Jesus, when I don't know how or when the load is too heavy, it strengthens me to know that you _____.

» Lord, help us look to you when feelings of inadequacy come, especially how you are _____. I pray specifically that my pastor may see you as _____.

AN EXPERIENCE OF SCRIPTURE

So the LORD must wait for you to come to him
so he can show you his love and compassion.

—ISAIAH 30:18

» God, I am coming to you with my own feelings of inadequacy. I need you to show me your love and compassion because _____.

» Let us come boldly before your throne and ask for help. Let us experience your love and compassion in fresh, new ways. I also pray that my pastor would enjoy _____.

ENGAGING GOD'S PEOPLE

Affirm your pastor's strengths in written or spoken words. Everyone can benefit from more reminders about the things they do well.

CLAIM HIS PROMISES

There is no one like the God of Israel.
    He rides across the heavens to help you,
    across the skies in majestic splendor.

—Deuteronomy 33:26

Love the Lord 3:
A Spirit-empowered disciple loves the Lord through experiencing God as He really is through deepened intimacy with Him.

Day 7

SPIRITUAL RISK

Let our *love for the Lord* be strengthened, refreshed, and renewed. Let us enjoy spiritual, emotional, and mental health. Let us regularly hear from you about any personal needs for nurture or care.

More than nine out of ten pastors rate themselves at a medium or low spiritual risk. Pastors report that their own spiritual nurture is provided through peers, mentors, worship, and spiritual disciplines. We can celebrate that our ministry leaders know the key ingredients that God has provided for spiritual, emotional, and mental health.

Just as we can celebrate pastors' perspectives of spiritual risk, we must also join them in guarding against another risk that threatens their health. Fifty-five percent of US adults report either some or frequent times of exhaustion, while 75 percent of pastors report some or frequent times of physical weariness and emotional fatigue.

STORIES FROM A PASTOR'S HEART

"I guess I just care too much." That was Anthony's frequent conclusion as he found himself exhausted and burned out from ministry demands. Anthony's family and elder board encouraged him to take some much-needed time away with the Lord.

It was a special encounter with Jesus that enabled Anthony to let go of some of the ministry stress. As he spent time in prayer and listened to the Lord, it was almost as if Jesus whispered to Anthony's soul: "Do the things that only you can do. I'm giving you the courage to say no. Let go of some of the responsibilities, so that we can have more times of refreshment together. I've been caring for these people long *before* you noticed them, and I'll be caring for them long *after* you've moved on. Trust me with the people you serve. Join me in loving them well—it will be enough!" This special moment of listening to God brought new perspective, more joy, more courage, and less exhaustion.

A FRESH ENCOUNTER WITH JESUS

I don't want you to be exhausted. I am here, waiting to refresh the weary. If you will come to me, I will give you rest and renew your strength. Get into the yoke of ministry with me, and I'll show you how to care for people without burning out. Learn from me. I've been loving people for a long time. Together, we can serve others well (see Jeremiah 31:25 NIV; Matthew 11:28).

» Jesus, show me how I can join you in loving others, so that I'm less vulnerable to burn out. Reveal any commitments that I need to set aside.

» Lord, refresh and satisfy us. Give us rest where there is weariness. Reveal any areas where we need to courageously say no. I pray specifically that you would give my pastor _____.

AN EXPERIENCE OF SCRIPTURE

Serve only the LORD your God ... Obey his commands, listen to his voice, and cling to him.

—DEUTERONOMY 13:4

» God, I want to listen to you. I'm clinging to you and your wisdom. What do you want me to know about the demands of my life? In what ways do you want to strengthen me?

» Empower us to get away from the demands of ministry and listen to you. Help us cling to you for spiritual, physical, and emotional health. I pray my pastor would enjoy _____.

ENGAGING GOD'S PEOPLE

Offer to help with tasks in the pastor's home or serve alongside your pastor in ministry. Ask if there are any demands of ministry that you could fill.

CLAIM HIS PROMISES

I listen carefully to what God the LORD is saying,
for he speaks peace to his faithful people.

—PSALM 85:8

Love the Lord 2:
A Spirit-empowered disciple loves the Lord through listening to and hearing God for direction and discernment.

PASTORAL INFLUENCE

> Allow our *love for the Lord* to be strengthened. Give us consistent times of rejoicing in the identity that we are God's beloved.

*M*ost of us see our pastor as someone who is practicing Christian values, and we look up to our leaders with great respect. In fact, 87 percent of church attendees indicate that they view their pastor positively and 44 percent esteem pastors as "very influential" in the community.

As members of the faith community, we also have an important opportunity. The aging of the church-attending population and the rise of the millennial generation is changing pastoral perceptions. Only 29 percent of millennials say pastors are a significant benefit in the community. The circumstances are right. Let's encourage and pray for our pastors to live out their God-given calling in fresh, relevant ways.

STORIES FROM A PASTOR'S HEART

For too many years, I struggled as a pastor. My biggest pressures were internal—I tried to please every member of our congregation. Essentially, that meant I went to work every day and reported to 200 different bosses! In order to please an elder, I changed the way I dressed. In order to satisfy a younger audience, we used church funds to buy completely unnecessary technology upgrades. We tried the latest programs. I altered my style of preaching—all because I was trying to keep the members happy.

My life and ministry began to look different the day I found myself on mandatory bed rest because of a heart attack. When you're that still, God's voice has a way of getting through. He spoke to me clearly: "You are my beloved. You are worthy of the gift of my Son. I bought your freedom, so I want you to be free. Be who I created you to be. Trust me with the outcomes."

I did what God said. I trusted Him and made it a priority to please Him. It was so much easier to please the one who already saw me as His "beloved." It was so much less pressure to "work for" the one who had already paid for my salvation. I was set free. Out of that freedom, God began to bring more courage and more confidence. The result was a more content pastor and a more secure congregation.

A FRESH ENCOUNTER WITH JESUS

I call you my beloved because you are so dear to me. Don't worry about what others think of you or put too much weight in their opinion. I created you and have declared you worth the gift of my Son. You are precious in my sight, and I love you. So rest easy in my love. Live boldly in your identity (see 1 John 3:1; 1 Corinthians 6:20; Isaiah 43:4).

» God, when I remember that you see me as your beloved, I feel _____.

» Lord, remind us daily that we are precious and worth the gift of your Son. Help us to live boldly in this identity. I pray my pastor would enjoy _____.

AN EXPERIENCE OF SCRIPTURE

To the praise of the glory of His grace, which He freely bestowed on us in the beloved.

—EPHESIANS 1:6 NASB

» God, I want to praise you for your glorious grace. I praise you for being a God who sees me through grace-filled lenses. I'm especially grateful for that because _____.

» Give us the grace to begin each day with a fresh reminder of the name you have given us—beloved. We praise you for every good and perfect gift. Help us see others as you see them. I pray my pastor would enjoy more _____.

ENGAGING GOD'S PEOPLE

Go through the Scriptures, reminding yourself of your identity in Christ. E-mail or text one of these Scriptures to your pastor each week.

CLAIM HIS PROMISES

For He gives to His beloved even in his sleep.

—PSALM 127:2 NASB

We give thanks to God always for all of you, making mention of you in our prayers; constantly bearing in mind your work of faith and labor of love and steadfastness of hope in our Lord Jesus Christ in the presence of our God and Father, knowing, brethren beloved by God, His choice of you …

—1 THESSALONIANS 1:2–4 NASB

Love the Lord 4:
A Spirit-empowered disciple loves the Lord by rejoicing regularly in his or her identity as His beloved.

Day 9

PASTORAL CALLING

Allow our *love for the Lord* to be demonstrated through bold, believing, and disciplined prayer.

*P*astors remain clear in their calling to shepherd God's people. In fact, 31 percent of church leaders report that they are just as confident today as when first called into ministry. An amazing 66 percent of pastors indicate they are even more confident of God's call now! It is likely that most ministry leaders sensed their calling and important direction from the Lord through prayer and reading Scripture.

As members of the household of faith, we rejoice over the confidence in calling that most pastors experience. But amid this confidence, roughly six out of ten pastors say they have felt "inadequate for their calling" during the past three months. It seems that the majority of ministry leaders are certain about God's call on their lives, but not as confident in their ability to live it out. It's also no surprise that pastors feel this sense of inadequacy most acutely when attendance of their church declines.

Let's lift our pastors in prayer, asking the Lord to help them return to bold, believing faith in the one who called them.

STORIES FROM A PASTOR'S HEART

Monday morning blues. Every pastor knows them. The Sunday sermon is done, and the adrenaline of weekend services has faded; it's then that evaluation sets in. How many "nickels and noses" can be counted? How was the sermon received? What impact or decisions were made? Even with a secure call into ministry, most pastors feel the pressure to perform. Sunday is the highpoint. Monday is often filled with examination, assessment, and second-guessing.

Pastors who learn to leave the Monday morning blues behind are the ones who allow the Holy Spirit to lead them into a bolder faith. They embrace the promise that "[he] who began the good work within you, will continue his work until it is finally finished on the day when Christ Jesus returns" (Philippians 1:6).

A FRESH ENCOUNTER WITH JESUS

Talk to me often! I lean in to listen to the needs of your heart. If you ask anything according to my will, I hear you, and you will have what you ask. I love it when you trust me. It brings me pleasure when you demonstrate faith in my power and love. Pray boldly. Pray constantly. Look for me to answer (see Psalm 4:3; 1 John 5:14–15; Ephesians 6:18; Jeremiah 33:3; Hebrews 11:6).

» Jesus, my heart is glad that you lean in to listen to my needs. I want to bring you pleasure, so I'm trusting you to _____.

» Lord, give us a bold faith. Help us pray to you boldly, constantly, and with expectant faith. I pray my pastor would experience more _____.

AN EXPERIENCE OF SCRIPTURE

And we are confident that he hears us whenever we ask for anything that pleases him … We also know that he will give us what we ask for.

—1 JOHN 5:14–15

» God, I am confident you hear me and you are pleased when I trust you. So I trust you to work in this area of my life _____.

» I'm confident it would please you for us to grow in boldness and faith. So I ask you to _____. I'm praying my pastor would enjoy more _____.

ENGAGING GOD'S PEOPLE

Ask your pastor what faith-stretching prayers he or she is praying. Commit to joining your pastor and looking for God to answer.

CLAIM HIS PROMISES

Call to Me and I will answer you …

—JEREMIAH 33:3 NASB

You faithfully answer our prayers with awesome deeds,
        O God our savior.

—PSALM 65:5

Love the Lord 8:
A Spirit-empowered disciple loves the Lord through disciplined, bold, and believing prayer.

PASTORAL WISDOM AND CREDIBILITY

Help our *love for the Lord* to be evident through frequent times of personal praise and worship.

The clear majority (69 percent) of individuals who claim the name of Jesus view their pastor as someone who is a reliable source for how to live out God's will. Additionally, 70 percent of Christians believe that their pastor knows and understands God's will for the world; 59 percent of believing Christians report that they see their pastor as someone who knows how relationships work and how to improve them. While it's a relief to know that congregation members have confidence in their leaders, that's a lot of pressure for a pastor!

To deal with the pressures of ministry, it will benefit our pastors to not only have the support of their congregation, but they'll also need increasing times of intimate conversation with the Lord. Unfortunately, only one in eight pastors say that worship is an essential discipline in their own spiritual growth. The pressure to discern and declare God's truth underscores the importance of pastors hearing from the Lord.

STORIES FROM A PASTOR'S HEART

Paula poured out her emptiness to Pastor Bill and vulnerably asked, "What do I need to do?" Paula and her husband, David, were near separation. She could feel the coldness growing. Paula had recently come to faith in Christ, but her husband wanted nothing to do with faith. The topic of church or faith or the pastor seemed to drive a deeper wedge between them.

During Bill's morning time with the Lord, he sensed the Lord saying, "Bill, this isn't about Paula and David's marriage. This is about his faith. Invite David to have coffee with you. Ask him about his experiences with me."

David had yet to put his faith in Jesus, but Bill knew it was only a matter of time.

Sometime later, David joined his wife on the front row of the Easter service, and they soon attended a marriage Bible study together.

Each morning, Bill prays for Paula and David and then listens to the Lord for what's next. His morning devotions are filled with praise for what God is doing in the life of this special couple. Bill's moments of worship begin with gratitude for God's faithfulness, guidance, and extravagant love.

A FRESH ENCOUNTER WITH JESUS

Remember, there is no one like me. I never forsake the ones who seek me. I want to be your ever-present teacher and your gentle guide. I will refresh and satisfy you if you're weary or tired. In fact, it pleases me to make you strong. The other thing that pleases me is a grateful heart. When we share moments of praise and thanksgiving, I feel honored (see Psalm 9:10; Isaiah 30:21; Proverbs 18:10; Jeremiah 31:25; Psalm 89:17).

» Jesus, I want to praise you and worship you today for _____.

» Lord, please draw us into more and more times of worship with you. May we honor you with personal moments of intimacy, gratitude, and praise. I pray my pastor would experience more.

AN EXPERIENCE OF SCRIPTURE

Bless the LORD, O my soul,
And all that is within me, bless His holy name.

—PSALM 103:1 NASB

» God, I bless your name with all that I am. Your name is great because you _____.

» Help us to come to you often in worship. May we find new ways to bless you. Give us the grace to prioritize time to declare the greatness of your name. I specifically pray for my pastor to experience more _____.

ENGAGING GOD'S PEOPLE

Ask your pastor how you might support him or her in more times of personal praise and worship. Discuss practical ideas and support your pastor in making this happen.

CLAIM HIS PROMISES

Happy are those who hear the joyful call to worship,
for they will walk in the light of your presence, LORD.

—PSALM 89:15

Yet a time is coming and has now come when the true worshipers will worship the Father in the Spirit and in truth, for they are the kind of worshipers the Father seeks. God is spirit, and his worshipers must worship in Spirit and in truth.

—JOHN 4:23–24

Love the Lord 7:
A Spirit-empowered disciple loves the Lord by entering often into Spirit-led praise and worship.

A SPIRIT-
EMPOWERED
DISCIPLE
lives the Word

Day 11

IT MAKES A DIFFERENCE

Help us *live the Word.* Let Scripture become real in our lives, vocation, and calling, that every person who encounters us will know God's Word makes a difference.

It is great to see that a vast majority (88 percent) of pastors assess their spiritual well-being as good or excellent. Additionally, when asked to identify some of their main goals for ministry, pastors listed the following objectives as being the most important:

- 36 percent of pastors said their goal was to be the hands and feet of Jesus,
- 22 percent of pastors desired to embody the kingdom of God, and
- 10 percent of a pastor's aim was to live in obedience to the teaching of Scripture.

Pastors' desires, intentions, and purposes are clearly in line with the challenge to live the Word of God.

While our pastors have a clear calling and sense of purpose, six out of ten pastors are at what researchers determined as a "medium risk" for spiritual difficulties. This statistic was based upon responses that indicate a pastor may have difficulty investing in his or her own spiritual development. This challenge provides us with a great opportunity to support our pastors so they can be more equipped to live out their purpose and calling from the Lord.

STORIES FROM A PASTOR'S HEART

Pastor Jeff became intrigued by how the church of the first century could impact their world for Jesus. As he prayed through the second chapter of Acts, the Holy Spirit seemed to point out this truth: There's power when God's people can say, "*This*, that you are seeing about my life, is simply *that* which is written about in Scripture" (see Acts 2:16). *This is that* became a sermon series and a theme throughout the church.

Jeff challenged his people to live out specific Bible verses in startling ways. For instance, members of the congregation didn't just talk about Matthew 25:40 and the importance of serving "the least of these." The congregation lived it out. Jeff led the teams that served the homeless, cared for the orphans, and ministered to teens who had been involved in sex trafficking. Whenever anyone would ask about their motive or how they were able to do such loving things, the answer was always this: "*This* love and care that you're seeing among our people, is just *that* Bible you've heard about. We're committed to living God's Book!"

A FRESH ENCOUNTER WITH JESUS

I love for you to hear my Word, but don't just listen to it. Do what it says. When you live out my Word, great things happen. You and I stay close and connected—I love that. My Word is a protection for you and the truth brings good to your life. Also, I feel loved when you live my Word (see James 1:22; John 15:10; 14:21; Deuteronomy 10:12–13).

» Jesus, when I reflect on the great things that happen when I live your Word, I feel grateful that _____. I want your Word to be evident in my life because _____.

» Give us a fresh passion for preaching your Word, but also for living it out. Help us demonstrate love for you by living out your Word in practical ways. Lord, give my pastor even more _____.

AN EXPERIENCE OF SCRIPTURE

The only letter of recommendation we need is you yourselves …

—2 CORINTHIANS 3:2

» God, I want my life to be like a written recommendation for your Son. Help me to:

- acknowledge my sin and apologize quickly (see James 5:16),

- encourage others who are discouraged (see 1 Thessalonians 5:11),

- give preference to others (see Romans 12:10), and

- pursue peace with others (Romans 14:19).

» In the same way, allow us to be a written recommendation for you, especially in these ways: _____. Lord, give my pastor even more moments of _____.

ENGAGING GOD'S PEOPLE

Write your pastor a note, affirming ways you have observed him or her living out God's Word.

CLAIM HIS PROMISES

But I lavish unfailing love for a thousand generations on those who love me and obey my commands.

—Deuteronomy 5:10

Live the Word 2:
A Spirit-empowered disciple lives the Word by being a living epistle, as His Word becomes real in life, vocation, and calling.

LIVE IN HUMILITY

> Help us *live the Word* by demonstrating humility. Enable us to be vulnerable, approachable, and always ready to share areas of growth or needed change.

*E*ffective leadership requires that a leader become teachable, hearing and learning from others. At times, the most effective leaders are even willing to change their perspective. Gratefully, 92 percent of pastors indicate that they have a willingness to hear others' opinions, even when those opinions differ from their own. Additionally, 84 percent of pastors affirm what is often called an "intellectual humility" or display an openness to change their minds. Let's look for opportunities to celebrate our pastors' approachability and openness to listen.

While most ministry leaders indicate a willingness to hear others' opinions and affirm their intellectual humility, there are some obstacles for pastors. Overconfidence and feeling threatened when others disagree can hinder a pastor from demonstrating humility. These obstacles were confirmed when three out of ten pastors indicated that they believe their ideas are usually better than most. Additionally, when a ministry leader fails to separate his or her ideas or perspective from his or her own personal worth or importance, that person can be hindered in his or her approachability. Again, three out of ten pastors feel threatened when others disagree with them on a topic close to their heart. Let's pray for a secure identity and a humble heart for our ministry leaders.

STORIES FROM A PASTOR'S HEART

I should have seen it coming, but I was blinded by my own "success." I'm a passionate, enthusiastic, and driven guy. God gifted me with a natural ability to lead and blessed me with a passion for getting things done. So, when the church was growing and people were coming to faith in Christ, ministry looked pretty perfect. When we had relational connections in the city that meant growing influence and impact, it didn't seem like ministry could get any better. Until one day, my mentor had some words that put these "great things" into focus.

We sat in the restaurant, catching up on events of the week, when Bill turned to me and asked, "How long has it been since you've shared some of your failures or ways you need to grow and change?" Bill went on to say, "Because I love you, I need to say this: Things are good, but almost dangerously good. I'm worried that you're distracting others from the one whom all of this is about—Jesus."

After that lunch, we regularly pray this simple prayer together, which has had a profound impact on my life and ministry: "Lord Jesus, I want you to look at my life and show me any actions, attitudes, or ideas that distract me from you. Please show me how you want me to change. Please bring people into my life to point out these growth areas because I want to experience and express your humility" (see Matthew 11:28–29).

A FRESH ENCOUNTER WITH JESUS

Humble yourself, and I will lift you up. I love it when you acknowledge your dependence on me. In fact, I can't wait to rescue

*those who come to me in humility. I am ready to teach you my
ways and lead you in how to do the right things. Your humility is
what moves me to action. I keep my distance from the proud. So,
talk freely about how you need me and how you are depending
upon me (see James 4:10; Psalm 18:27; 25:9; 69:32; 138:6).*

» Jesus, I am grateful my humility brings your promise of
rescue. So today, I declare my dependence on you about
_____.

» Lord, empower us with a humble spirit that readily
shares about how you are working and bringing change
to life and ministry. I pray my pastor would enjoy more
_____.

AN EXPERIENCE OF SCRIPTURE

*Always be humble and gentle. Be patient with each other,
making allowance for each other's faults because of your love.*

—EPHESIANS 4:2

» God, I ask that you help me be more humble and gentle with _____. Help me to make allowance for their
faults because you have loved me despite mine.

» Equip us with humility and gentleness. Help us make
allowances for others' faults because we sense your
great love for us in the midst of our faults. Lord, give my
pastor even more moments of _____.

ENGAGING GOD'S PEOPLE

Affirm your pastor for demonstrations of humility and vulnerability. Communicate your gratitude for this Christlike
example.

CLAIM HIS PROMISES

The humble will see their God at work and be glad.
Let all who seek God's help be encouraged.

—PSALM 69:32

Humble yourselves in the presence of the Lord, and He will exalt you.

—JAMES 4:10 NASB

Live the Word 4:
A Spirit-empowered disciple lives the Word by humbly and vulnerably sharing of the Spirit's transforming work through the Word.

Day 13

LIVING FINANCIALLY CONFIDENT

Allow us to *live the Word*. Give us unwavering trust in God's promise to supply all our needs in Christ Jesus.

The majority of ministry leaders are satisfied with their financial status. Research indicates that while the median income for full-time pastors ($63,000) was approximately 10 percent below comparably educated US adults in other fields ($71,000), an amazing 95 percent of pastors are satisfied with their vocation and perceived their financial security as stable, secure, or having a surplus. Their financial confidence may come less from their bank account and more from their faith in God's provision for those He calls. Let's celebrate their confidence in God and His Word.

While we can celebrate that most pastors feel satisfied with their financial status, almost one in three pastors feel unprepared for unseen expenses (31 percent). Additionally, we must remember that small church pastors and bi-vocational pastors more commonly report "surviving or struggling" in their financial security. Let's be sure to lift our pastors in prayer and claim God's provision for them and their families.

STORIES FROM A PASTOR'S HEART

Shawn and Jayla are among the courageous ministry leaders who have sensed God's call to plant a church in hard-to-reach places. Making the move was a challenge, but the finances of their move required a special step of faith. Planting a congregation meant leaving the financial security and regular salary of their church in Alabama to start a new body of believers in California. Nothing about the move made sense, but the couple was certain of God's call.

Before Shawn and Jayla made their move, their home church challenged the new congregation to look for ways to bless their pastor. They were encouraged to see themselves as "owners" of the vision, not just members of a church. Just as a homeowner would do, members were asked to look for ways to give to their pastor each month. For most families, this meant monthly financial contributions, but many provided in other ways. Some shared babysitting services so Shawn and Jayla didn't have to pay for childcare. Others offered their vacation homes so the pastor and family could look forward to a low-cost getaway for the summer.

There were certainly financial challenges along the journey, but Shawn, Jayla, and their congregation have now seen God grow their vision, their church, and their faith. As always, God was faithful to His calling and His promise to provide. (For more information about practical ways to bless your pastor, see greatcommandment.net.)

A FRESH ENCOUNTER WITH JESUS

Few things are more stressful than financial need. Those are the times when I want you to come to me. I am your security, not a bank account. I made the promise to provide for all your needs, and I am faithful to keep it. Trust me. Manage your finances with integrity, ask for my help, and give generously. Trust me com-

pletely, then look for how I will provide (see Philippians 4:19; Proverbs 3:26; Philippians 4:11; 1 Timothy 6:10; Deuteronomy 15:10–11).

» Jesus, I trust you to meet my need for _____. Help me be content in _____.

» Lord, empower us to trust you with financial concerns, especially regarding _____. Meet _____ (this need) for us. For my pastor's needs, I pray you would _____.

AN EXPERIENCE OF SCRIPTURE

If you free your heart of greed, showing compassion and true generosity to the poor … you will be clean within.

—LUKE 11:41 TPT

» God, reveal any areas of greed or any additional ways I can show generosity to others. Show me how I can trust you more.

» Help us see any areas of needed growth in financial matters. May we be true examples of generosity and trust in you. I pray my pastor would enjoy more _____.

ENGAGING GOD'S PEOPLE

Support adequate salary, insurance, and retirement plans for your pastor. You might also share your time, talents, resources, or friendships.

CLAIM HIS PROMISES

Oh, fear the LORD, you his saints,
*   for those who fear him have no lack!*

The young lions suffer want and hunger;
but those who seek the LORD lack no good thing.

—PSALM 34:9–10 ESV

And this same God who takes care of me will supply all your
needs from his glorious riches, which have been given to us
in Christ Jesus.

—PHILIPPIANS 4:19

If you free your heart of greed, showing compassion and true
generosity to the poor, you have more than clean hands, you
will be clean within.

—LUKE 11:41 TPT

Live the Word 10:
A Spirit-empowered disciple lives the Word by demonstrating an implicit, unwavering trust that God's Word will never fail.

Day 14

BIBLICAL RELEVANCE

Help us *live the Word*. Let the Scriptures be hidden away in our hearts; help us to enjoy frequent moments of meditation in God's Word.

Surveys of US adults provide encouraging news on the topics they find most valuable for pastors to address. One in four adults indicates they are interested in biblical values, like caring for the poor, honesty, integrity, sacrificial giving, and serving others. One in five adults expresses interest in family issues. Let's celebrate our pastors' emphasis on biblical values and family needs. Gratefully, pastors can be reassured that when preaching on these topics, they are preaching with relevance and providing hope for our homes. Interest in these topics also informs us about pathways for sharing the gospel.

Scripture presents five different ways we can relate to the Word of God. We can hear, read, and study God's Word. And we can also memorize and meditate on Scripture. Pastors report a steady diet of hearing, reading, and studying the Scriptures, but only 7 percent of pastors note Scripture memory as an important spiritual discipline. Only 13 percent of our ministry leaders indicate that silence and solitude are important for their spiritual journey.

Let's pray that our pastors will recommit to not only hearing, reading, and studying God's Word, but also to memorization and meditation. May they be *fully* equipped to accurately handle the word of truth (see 2 Timothy 2:15).

STORIES FROM A PASTOR'S HEART

My pastor is known for his wisdom. He has a reputation for knowing just what to say in the most challenging situations. When faced with important decisions, Pastor Jeff knows how to direct you. When bombarded with hard questions, he confidently guides you to the biblical truth you most need. It took me several years, but I finally realized the secret to my pastor's wisdom. His secret? Morning walks.

Pastor Jeff and I live in the same neighborhood. Every day, I see him going out for his morning walk. Previously, I thought that those walks were all about physical health and fitness. I now know Jeff's walks are about much more. About seven o'clock each morning, my pastor can be seen walking through the neighborhood, phone in hand, earphones in place.

One day I was curious, so I asked Jeff what kind of music he listens to while he walks. Here was his reply: "I don't listen to music very often. I'm usually listening to my Bible app. I ask the Lord every month which passages of Scripture He wants me to memorize, and then I walk. I walk while I read, listen to, and memorize those verses. When I think I've got it, I record myself saying those verses into my phone. Then I just meditate, asking the Lord to show me fresh things from His Word. You know—He always does."

A FRESH ENCOUNTER WITH JESUS

Your days are filled with constant stress and distraction, but time with me can replace those moments with peace. Hold firmly to my words, for they'll bring you life. Guard my words as your most precious possession. Keep them in your heart, because knowing and meditating on my Word will help you resist temptation, help you make wise decisions, and give you strength and comfort. All these are my gifts, ready and waiting just for you (see Psalm 4:4; 46:10; 119:105; Jeremiah 15:16b; Psalm 119:49–50).

» Jesus, I want to give more priority to memorizing and meditating on your words because _____.

» Lord, I ask you to impress us with the need to meditate on and memorize your words, so that we experience more _____. I pray my pastor would enjoy more _____.

AN EXPERIENCE OF SCRIPTURE

I will meditate on all Your work
And muse on Your deeds.

—Psalm 77:12 NASB

» God, I want to be still before you and reflect on the ways you have worked in my life. Help me see and remember the special ways you have acted on my behalf.

» Lord, enable us to reflect on your deeds, meditate on your acts, and then express gratitude for them. I pray my pastor would enjoy more _____.

ENGAGING GOD'S PEOPLE

Provide your pastor with a gift of music, Scripture memory resources, or time away for solitude. Encourage your pastor with practical tools for meditation and memorization.

CLAIM HIS PROMISES

This book of the law shall not depart from your mouth, but you shall meditate on it day and night, so that you may be careful to do according to all that is written in it; for then you will make your way prosperous, and then you will have success.

—Joshua 1:8 NASB

Guard my words as your most precious possession. Write them down, and also keep them deep within your heart.

—Proverbs 7:2–3 TLB

 Live the Word 5:
A Spirit-empowered disciple lives the Word by meditating consistently on more and more of the Word.

Day 15

LIVING LIKE JESUS

> Help us *live the Word*. Characterize us as ones who live like Jesus.

*W*hen ministry leaders were asked to describe the traits of a good pastor, their most often listed qualities were patience and prayer, humility and compassion, calling and integrity. Without realizing it, pastors listed many of the significant qualities in the life of Jesus. Let's celebrate that our leaders' hearts are in alignment with the Savior's heart. Their desire and goal are to live and minister like Jesus.

While we celebrate that our pastors' view of an effective leader aligns so closely with Jesus, we must also consider the role of pastors and how they are seen more broadly. Unfortunately, only 24 percent of all US adults say their opinion of pastors in general is "very positive." This number soars to 64 percent of adults viewing pastors as "very positive" when they come to know a pastor personally. These statistics call us to pray for our pastors' ability to engage in the community, calling upon the Lord to bring greater opportunities to relate to others outside the church. May our pastors live and love like Jesus in their community, and then lead us to do the same.

STORIES FROM A PASTOR'S HEART

The entire European tour was memorable, but it was the experience at the Cambridge University campus that Corey and Jana will never forget. They stood in the middle of student square, teaching students about the reliability of the resurrection and the authority of the Bible. Some students seemed reassured by the truth; others were combative. Yet during these rational arguments about matters of the faith, one girl stood up and asked a more relational question: "Based upon these convictions of yours, you're telling us it's important to live like Jesus. Well, Jesus fed the poor and healed the sick. So please tell us what you have done for the homeless lately?"

The girl's question was sincere and full of genuine interest. It wasn't asked in sarcasm or with malicious intent. Because of a young lady's wholehearted concern that day, Corey and Jana felt the Holy Spirit's conviction. They realized that they had embraced the truth of Jesus, but their relationship with Him needed to translate into more and more ways of living and loving like Him. Lives were changed on campus that day. Pastors Corey and Jana had no idea their ministry trip to Europe would be such a moment of life-changing ministry for them.

A FRESH ENCOUNTER WITH JESUS

Remember those childhood games where one person would try to mirror or imitate the exact movements of another? That game works beautifully for you and me. If you'll watch closely and carefully consider the way I lived on earth, you'll notice one theme—love. Notice how I loved the Father and cared for other people—walk in that same love. And don't worry, for I have a promise for you: If you love me, you'll keep my commandments (see Ephesians 5:1–2; John 14:15).

» Jesus, remind me of some of the extravagant ways you loved. I want to carefully consider how you loved me. Help me notice, Lord, _____.

» Give us a fresh experience of your love today. Help us see new dimensions of your love with each sermon, Bible study, or time of prayer. I pray also that my pastor would enjoy more _____.

AN EXPERIENCE OF SCRIPTURE

Therefore be imitators of God, as beloved children. And walk in love …

—Ephesians 5:1–2 ESV

» God, help me to be a better imitation of you. Show me how you want me to imitate you and your love.

» Empower us to be a mirror of you and then walk with that same love for others. I also pray that you would give my pastor _____.

ENGAGING GOD'S PEOPLE

Talk to your pastor about the new dimensions of love that you've carefully considered and are beginning to practice. Let your pastor see your commitment to imitating Jesus.

CLAIM HIS PROMISES

If you love Me, you will keep My commandments.

—John 14:15 NASB

For to this you have been called, because Christ also suffered for you, leaving you an example, so that you might follow in his steps.

—1 Peter 2:21 ESV

Live the Word 2:

A Spirit-empowered disciple lives the Word by being a living epistle, as His Word becomes real in life, vocation, and calling.

FREE FROM PAINFUL EMOTIONS

Help us *live the Word*. Free us from feelings of anger, fear, sadness, guilt, disappointment, and depression. Allow us to experience God's healing and freedom from every painful emotion.

As individuals who care about pastors, it's important to know that nearly half of all ministry leaders (46 percent) report struggling with depression during their ministry tenure. Gratefully, only a small percentage leaves the ministry due to this struggle. A pastor who deals with emotional challenges openly and vulnerably is a pastor who is increasingly wise and compassionate with people. Let's celebrate the times when our shepherds are emotionally free and readily show compassion for others.

When ministry satisfaction is low, or if attendance declines, many ministry leaders can experience depression. Increased stress and overwhelming pressure make depression also more common among pastors of smaller churches. Church members' sensitivity to these opportunities for compassion and encouragement are important. Pastors need our support, care, compassion, and encouragement. They don't need our criticism, judgment, or "constructive advice." When pastors were surveyed about the communication received from their members, 77 percent was deemed helpful and 15 percent unhelpful. Let's pray for and practice helpful communication with our pastors.

STORIES FROM A PASTOR'S HEART

After a long season of extreme ministry pressure and at the insistence of his wife, Mark decided to finally see a Christian counselor and family physician for his depression. Mark was prescribed medication that helped reestablish healthy sleep patterns and stabilize his mood. He was also shocked to learn that his problem was not just a loss of passion, but that for a very long time he had not stopped to feel much at all.

During their sessions, Mark and his counselor took the time to find the feelings beneath the depression. Mark shared feelings of hurt, disappointment, anxiety, anger, guilt, and grief with the therapist and with the Lord. It became clear that these unresolved painful emotions had left little room for joy, peace, gratitude, or love. As he began to experience the scriptures God ordained for healing each of these emotions, Mark's passion returned. God's healing was evident.

Life's pain is inevitable. Let's pray for our pastors to experience God's abundant freedom, healing, and provision.

A FRESH ENCOUNTER WITH JESUS

If you are struggling with sadness, discouragement, or defeat, come to me and let my unfailing love surround and comfort you. Pour out your heart to me, because I promise to hear you and deliver you from your troubles. I not only care about the anguish of your soul; it makes my heart sing to give you strength. Because you are the one I love, I will refresh you when you're weary, and I will satisfy you when you are faint (see Psalm 32:10; 62:8; 2 Corinthians 1:3–4; Psalm 31:7; 34:17; 89:17; Jeremiah 31:25).

» Jesus, I feel grateful to know that you _____. It comforts my heart to know that _____.

» Lord, I ask you to protect us from feelings of discouragement or depression. If we experience these emotions, let your comfort be very real to us. I pray also for my pastor, that you would _____.

AN EXPERIENCE OF SCRIPTURE

The righteous cry out, and the LORD hears them;
he delivers them from all their troubles.
—PSALM 34:17

» God, I cry out to you because _____. I need you to deliver me from _____. God, act quickly on our behalf.

» God, I cry out for my pastor as well. I pray that you would _____.

ENGAGING GOD'S PEOPLE

Ask the Lord to help you be aware of any times when your pastor may experience disappointment, discouragement, or depression. With the Lord's guidance, take practical steps needed to support your pastor.

CLAIM HIS PROMISES

The LORD himself goes before you and will be with you; he will never leave you nor forsake you. Do not be afraid; do not be discouraged.
—DEUTERONOMY 31:8

The righteous cry out, and the LORD hears them;
he delivers them from all their troubles.
—PSALM 34:17

You will make known to me the path of life;
In Your presence is fullness of joy;
In Your right hand there are pleasures forever.

—Psalm 16:11 NASB

Live the Word 9:
A Spirit-empowered disciple lives out God's Word by living abundantly in the present as God's Word brings healing to hurt, anger, guilt, fear, and condemnation.

Day 7

LEADING LIKE JESUS

Help us *live the Word.* Allow us to shepherd the church with wisdom, kingdom priorities, and a heart of servant-leadership.

*O*ur pastors are becoming more resilient. While pastoral leadership is needed now more than ever before, the complexities of cultural reconstruction, technological advancements, and moral relativism make the pastoral calling more challenging. Research indicates we may be moving beyond the failed hope of celebrity or heroic leaders to embrace the need for resilient leaders. Let's pray our pastors become more and more like the sons of Issachar, who understood the times and knew what to do (see 1 Chronicles 12:32). Look for ways your pastor is growing in resilience and wisdom, and be sure to celebrate.

Research indicates that the term "self-leadership" summarizes the biggest challenge to effective pastoral leadership in our complex world. Effective leadership does not mean going it alone, but rather practicing a concentric circle model of ministry. Our pastors' greatest impact will come as they give priority to intimacy and identity with the one who has called them, rather than the calling itself. Second, pastors will have greatest impact as they make home and family a priority over their congregation. Third, pastors will see the greatest kingdom impact when they enlist the wisdom and accountability of mentors. And, finally, they will see the greatest impact when they engage their church in reaching the community and beyond—in that order.

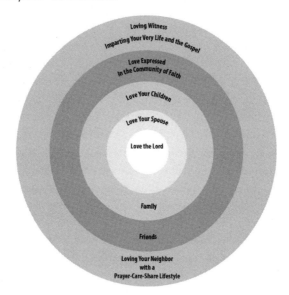

STORIES FROM A PASTOR'S HEART

Drew sat in David's office and shared his frustrations: "I've been trying to juggle all the demands of life, and it's not going well. As far as church is concerned, I feel like we must compete for time. I try to lead a relevant ministry, but it seems like our congregation gives priority to everything else but God."

David asked about family next. Drew's response was much the same: "Things at home aren't going much better. Kara went back to work this year so our finances wouldn't be so tight. We do the best we can to juggle family responsibilities, but it gets really nuts on those nights when I'm needed at the church or if a crisis happens with a church member. I don't feel like I'm a successful husband, father, or pastor these days."

After some thoughtful listening, David asked, "How long has it been since you've experienced a fresh encounter with Jesus? Drew, your frustrations are in part because you're trying to balance it all. That will never work. Think about the priorities of your life like the concentric circles that form when a stone is dropped into the water. Your first priority is to spend time with Jesus. Your next priority is your marriage and family, with church and community as final priorities. So, let's spend some time with the Lord. Jesus is a great high priest who understands, and He wants to bear these burdens with you."

A FRESH ENCOUNTER WITH JESUS

When you are called to lead or serve, I am right beside you. Be strong. Take courage. Know that I am with you, just like I was with Moses and Joshua. Remember, not everyone will always like you, but make a priority of pleasing me. When that's your priority, even your enemies will be at peace with you. And whatever you wish others would do for you, do for them. I came into the world to serve, not to be the boss. Take your cues from me. Leadership means looking for ways to serve (see Proverbs 16:7; Deuteronomy 31:23; Joshua 3:7; Matthew 7:12; Mark 10:42–45).

» Jesus, thank you for your promise of presence. Help me demonstrate a heart of service.

» Lord, empower us with the confidence of your presence. Give us the boldness of Joshua, the resilience of Moses, and the servant mindset of the Savior. I pray you would give my pastor a special sense of _____.

AN EXPERIENCE OF SCRIPTURE

Do nothing from selfish ambition or conceit, but in humility count others more significant than yourselves.

—Philippians 2:3 ESV

» God, show me how I might serve others and consider them more significant than myself.

» Let us lead with humility, seeing others as more significant than ourselves. Reassure us that our priority is you, so we are free to serve. I pray specifically for my pastor, that you would _____.

ENGAGING GOD'S PEOPLE

Ask your pastors how you might support their times away with the Lord, date nights, family time, ministry initiatives, and missional engagement.

CLAIM HIS PROMISES

And we all, with unveiled face, beholding the glory of the Lord, are being transformed into the same image from one degree of glory to another.

—2 Corinthians 3:18 ESV

Commit your way to the Lord;
*   trust in him, and he will act.*

—Psalm 37:5 ESV

Live the Word 6:
A Spirit-empowered disciple lives His Word by encountering Jesus in Scripture for deepened transformation in Christlikeness.

A SPIRIT-
EMPOWERED
DISCIPLE
Loves People

Day 18

LOVING PEOPLE

Deepen our *love for people*. God, overwhelm us by your love so that we can't help but give that kind of love to others.

*R*esearch tells us that most of us name one quality as the most important for the effectiveness of a pastor. What's that quality? Loving people! This is great news. Not all pastors have the same zeal, charisma, or great vision, and every pastor's leadership and preaching style is different. Yet every pastor can be great at loving people!

While congregants view "loving people" as the most important quality of an effective pastor, pastors themselves indicate that they may feel inadequate to meet the needs of the people they serve. Twenty-nine percent of pastors say they sometimes feel unprepared in helping people solve problems, and twenty-seven percent feel unprepared to handle conflict. This is an opportunity for God to equip and empower pastors so they're prepared to love people well.

STORIES FROM A PASTOR'S HEART

We started a church more than twenty years ago. With seventeen of our faithful friends, my wife and I followed the Lord's calling to plant a church in a suburban community of Arizona. God has been faithful to lead and provide. The church now reaches thousands and makes an eternal impact on our community. When asked about our success, we simply remember how it all began.

I had a routine of "startling love." Every Friday morning, I would drive to work and ask the Lord, "Who should I startle with love today?" By the time I got to the office, I had a list of names. I would begin making phone calls. "Ann, this is Pastor Roger. I was on my way to work this morning and remembered your faithfulness and how much I appreciate your leadership in the preschool ministry. I'm just calling to say thanks on behalf of countless parents and kids whom you've loved well for so many years." Or, "Jose, this is Pastor Roger. I drove into work today and was thinking about what an incredible job you do in coordinating our mission trips every year. You serve with compassion and excellence. Many lives are changed because of you."

I'm convinced it was those phone calls and the priority of loving people well that formed the foundation of a loving congregation and now a loving impact in our community. And it all started with my own experience of God's startling love for me.

A FRESH ENCOUNTER WITH JESUS

Remember, anyone who puts their hope and trust in me can count on my blessings. Watch for my good and perfect gifts. I have lots of them in store for you today (see Jeremiah 24:6–7; Lamentations 3:24–26; James 1:17).

» Jesus, we want to see your blessings. Help us notice the ways you surprise us with your love so that we can share that love with others.

» Open our eyes to see and experience your good and perfect blessings, so we can startle others with your love. Give my pastor even more moments of _____.

AN EXPERIENCE OF SCRIPTURE

Be generous with the different things God gave you, passing them around so all get in on it.

—1 PETER 4:10 MSG

» God, I'm especially grateful for your gifts of _____. Show me the people who need to be startled with this same kind of love. Help me to pass these gifts around.

» Allow us to see the people who need to be startled with your love. Empower us to be generous with your love and pass those gifts around so that you receive glory. I pray my pastor would experience even more _____.

ENGAGING GOD'S PEOPLE

Startle your pastor with his or her favorite snack or drink. Surprise your pastor with a note of appreciation, or brag on your pastor in front of other members. Startle your pastor with an affirming call.

CLAIM HIS PROMISES

Give, and you will receive. Your gift will return to you in full—pressed down, shaken together to make room for more, running over, and poured into your lap. The amount you give will determine the amount you get back.

—LUKE 6:38

Love People 2:
A Spirit-empowered disciple loves people by startling them with loving initiatives and giving first.

Day 19

PRIORITY
OF MARRIAGE

Deepen our *love for people.* Empower us to love the people closest to us, especially our spouse.

We can celebrate this truth: Most married pastors say they are satisfied in their relationships with their spouse (70 percent). It's important not to miss the good news of this truth. Thankfully, most of our ministry leaders are content with their marriage relationship. With all the demands on our pastors, we certainly want their marriage to be a relationship that thrives and serves as a place of peace and refuge.

There is an occupational hazard that comes with being a pastor. Someone always needs them. There are always church members who need care, counsel, wisdom, and direction. At the same time, there will *always* be people outside the church who need the gospel. Those demands and needs create unique pressures for every pastor.

A pastor who says yes to all the ministry needs often says no to his spouse and kids. It's no wonder then, when asked if they struggled with significant marital problems during their ministry, 26 percent of pastors said yes, while another 27 percent indicated substantial parenting difficulties as well.

STORIES FROM A PASTOR'S HEART

I'll never forget the day when my husband drove into the church parking lot, took my hand, and told me that the district superintendent was inside. "They are charging me with inappropriate behavior and immoral actions," he said. Shock and fear gripped my heart. Our marriage was in crisis, our family shaken. We would have to leave our parsonage; the kids would lose their friends. Relationships in our church family would be severed or strained at best. All security was gone.

When a ministry marriage struggles, the stakes are high and the consequences broad. God has since redeemed our marriage and our ministry, my husband's priorities have changed, and never again will I take our relationship for granted.

* * *

Our oldest son lost his battle with cancer. We really thought that we had mourned the loss, so we stepped back into ministry as usual. We were committed to serving our denomination overseas, and we were called to fulfill the Great Commission. So my spouse and I packed our belongings and our emotions and moved to Turkey.

When I realized that my spouse was struggling with depression, I knew ministry had to look different. Yes, I was sad not to be serving the people of Turkey. But you know what? The Great Commandment comes *before* the Great Commission. Therefore, my spouse comes before ministry. God is healing our hearts and sustaining our marriage. I'm not sure that would have been possible if I hadn't prioritized my marriage over ministry.

A FRESH ENCOUNTER WITH JESUS

I love the relationship between husband and wife. I created marriage to be a beautiful representation of me. Your best hope of creating a marriage that looks like me is if we partner together to love your spouse. Kneel alongside me and let's love your partner well (Romans 12:10, Philippians 2:7).

» Lord, enlighten and empower me in a fresh way, to love my spouse by following your example of humility, initiative, and sacrifice. Remind me to love my spouse and prioritize my marriage in ways that show I'm following you. I specifically pray that _____.

» Lord, I pray for my pastor's marriage. I pray specifically that you would _____.

AN EXPERIENCE OF SCRIPTURE

But I am among you as the one who serves.

—LUKE 22:27 ESV

» God, as I give time, energy, attention, and priority to my spouse, strengthen this relationship so we are better equipped to live out the calling you have given. I also pray for _____.

» God, I pray you would give my pastor and spouse even more _____.

ENGAGING GOD'S PEOPLE

Look for an opportunity to support your pastor and his or her relationship with his or her spouse. Offer to provide childcare while your pastor and spouse go on a date. Offer to go on a hospital visit or care for a church member so your pastor is free to prioritize family.

CLAIM HIS PROMISES

Your wife will be like a fruitful grapevine,
*   flourishing within your home. ...*
That is the LORD's blessing
*   for those who fear him.*

—PSALM 128:3–4

Summing up: Be agreeable, be sympathetic, be loving, be compassionate, and be humble. That goes for all of you, no exceptions. No retaliation. No sharp-tongued sarcasm. Instead, bless—that's your job, to bless. You'll be a blessing and get a blessing.

—1 PETER 3:8–9 MSG

Love People 5:
A Spirit-empowered disciple loves people by ministering His life and love to our nearest ones at home and with family, as well as faithful engagement in His body, the church.

Day 20

PASTORS AS PARENTS

Deepen our *love for people*. Strengthen our relationship with our children.

*O*ur pastors are resilient. As many as 27 percent of them report they have experienced parenting problems during their ministry, but faith in the direction of our heavenly Father guides them through the challenges of raising children. This resilience is evident when pastors rate their relationship with their children higher than the national average, with 60 percent of pastors indicating their relationship with their children is "excellent" and 36 percent reporting the relationship as "good."

Pastors are resilient, but let's not forget that almost half of pastors (48 percent) say that ministry has been "difficult on their family." The most common parenting regret among (42 percent) pastors was that they wished they had spent more time with their kids. These ministry leaders wished for more ministry-family balance, less travel, and more day-to-day involvement with their family. The pressures of a ministry family are intense. It's our privilege as ones who pray and care for pastors to come alongside them, offering compassion and practical support.

STORIES FROM A PASTOR'S HEART

My son, Nathan, begged me for days to take him to the toy store. His birthday money was burning a hole in his pocket. Saturday morning rolled around, and just as we were heading out the door, the phone rang. A church member's relative had been taken to the hospital and the family needed me. I kept my promise to go to the toy store that day, but I grieve every time I remember how the day ended. As we left the store, Nathan's words hit me hard. His voice was gentle, but here's what he said: "Thanks for taking me. Next time, maybe you'll *want* to be there."

* * *

For more than a decade, Thursday nights were "Family Nights" in our household. I came home early from the church, we turned off the phones, and we had dinner as a family. After dinner, our three kids would take turns selecting the fun activity for the evening. This meant that every few weeks, the kids knew it was going to be their turn again to choose the activity for Family Night. My wife and youngest daughter always selected outdoor fun—soccer, bike riding, or playing at the park. When it was our turn, my oldest daughter and I chose indoor fun. We didn't really like to sweat, so on our weeks, the family would be playing cards or board games. Our son could be counted on to choose charades—always charades.

While those Thursday night memories seem simple, we now realize they were powerful. These nights anchored our family. They solidified our relationships. They confirmed the priority of family over ministry.

A FRESH ENCOUNTER WITH JESUS

There's nothing stronger than a parent's love for his or her child. In fact, I see that love every time our Father looks at you. I also see the joy in your face when you take time to truly see your own children. Children are some of the Father's most precious gifts, so be sure to unwrap and admire them. Parenting is hard, so let me be your provider and guide. Just ask me for help, for I love to give it to you (see Psalm 127:3; 25:5; Matthew 7:11).

»   Jesus, help me to unwrap the gifts you have given me. What about my children do you want me to admire? What do you want me to see about their needs? Their future?

»   Lord, equip us to slow down and unwrap each of our children as gifts from the Lord. I pray for my pastor and pastor's children, that you would _____.

AN EXPERIENCE OF SCRIPTURE

Children are a gift from God; they are his reward.

—PSALM 127:3 TLB

»   Heavenly Father, you see my children as gifts and a reward. Help me see my children the way you see them. I pray specifically that _____.

ENGAGING GOD'S PEOPLE

Look for opportunities to help your pastor prioritize time with his or her children. Check in regularly to support family schedules. Help your pastor protect the family's calendar from ministry conflicts.

CLAIM HIS PROMISES

In the fear of the LORD one has strong confidence,
    and his children will have a refuge.

—PROVERBS 14:26 ESV

All your children shall be taught by the LORD,
　　and great shall be the peace of your children.

　　　　　　　　　　　　　　　　—ISAIAH 54:13 ESV

Children are a heritage from the LORD,
　　offspring a reward from him.
Like arrows in the hands of a warrior
　　are children in one's youth.
Blessed is the man
　　whose quiver is full of them.

　　　　　　　　　　　　　　　　—PSALM 127:3–5 NIV

Love People 5:
A Spirit-empowered disciple loves people by ministering His life and love to our nearest ones at home and with family, as well as faithful engagement in His body, the church.

Day 21

FRIENDSHIPS

Deepen our *love for people.* Allow us to enjoy deep, trusted friendships within the body of Christ.

Thankfully, 34 percent of pastors indicate their level of true friendships is "excellent," and 68 percent report they have experienced the support of friends in recent months. We can certainly celebrate the fact that healthy churches give their pastors freedom to *have friends*, both inside and outside the church.

While we celebrate that the majority of pastors report feeling supported by their friends, we can also pray through our concern that pastors are more likely (52 percent) than the general population (39 percent) to have experienced loneliness in the last three months. Let's pray for our pastors to develop close friendships. Trusted friendships are both preventative and restorative. Close relationships can prevent burnout, fatigue, and poor decisions. Trusted friends can also help restore a pastor's spiritual and emotional health when inevitable challenges come.

STORIES FROM A PASTOR'S HEART

Pastor Steve stood in his kitchen giving one more life lesson to his teenage son: "To have more friends, Kevin, you have to go around being a good friend." Kevin wasn't necessarily impacted by the nuggets of truth that day, but Steve certainly was.

As Steve prepared his next sermon, the Holy Spirit spoke to him. Jesus seemed to have close friends in ministry—Peter, James, and John shared the most intense ministry moments with the Savior. Jesus also had friends in the community—Mary, Martha, and Lazarus were clearly special friends of Jesus. He traveled out of His way to visit them, care for them, and share life with them. What struck Steve most poignantly was that Jesus had a reputation of being a friend. He was called a "friend of sinners."

The Holy Spirit prompted Steve with these thoughts: "Steve, I created you to need trusted people in your life. It's not good for you to be alone in ministry. So let's go around being a good friend. I know it's hard to let people in, but don't be afraid. I'll provide."

A FRESH ENCOUNTER WITH JESUS

I have never called you a servant; I call you my closest friend. I also created you to need people in your life. It's just not good for you to be alone in life or in ministry. The better wisdom is to find trusted, loyal friends—the ones who can help you in a time of need (see John 15:15; Genesis 2:18; Proverbs 17:17; 11:30).

» Jesus, I am grateful you offered me the gift of friendship. I'm thankful for your friendship because _____.

» God, provide us trusted friendships—one or two people who are willing and able to provide encouragement, support, loyalty, and accountability. Please give my pastor more and more friends who _____.

AN EXPERIENCE OF SCRIPTURE

As for me, I shall call upon God …

—PSALM 55:16 NASB

» Lord, I call upon you for help. You know how important it is to have trusted friends. Strengthen my friendships by helping me be a great friend to others.

» I call upon you, Lord, for empowerment and provision. Help us to be a good friend and provide us with friends who are committed to mutual care. I pray my pastor would enjoy more friends who _____.

ENGAGING GOD'S PEOPLE

Give your pastor freedom to have friends within the church, and encourage your pastor to establish friendships with ministry leaders in your city. These peer relationships are often some of the safest for your pastor. Provide any practical support that's needed to introduce or cultivate these friendships.

CLAIM HIS PROMISES

The seeds of good deeds become a tree of life;
a wise person wins friends.

—Proverbs 11:30

The heartfelt counsel of a friend
is as sweet as perfume and incense.

—Proverbs 27:9

Love People 3:
A Spirit-empowered disciple discerns the relational needs of others with a heart to give Christ's love.

DOES IT FIT?

> Deepen our *love for people*. Increase our sense of adequacy and empowerment to meet the growing needs of people.

*O*verall, it seems that the day-to-day tasks of a pastor fit his or her sweet spot. Fifty-five percent of pastors report that where they spend their time fits very well with their calling and giftedness. And since two-thirds of senior church leaders say they most enjoy preaching and teaching, we can celebrate the wisdom of churches who give their pastors freedom to make study and message preparation an important priority.

Interestingly, pastors seem to find pastoral counseling less of a fit for their natural giftedness and calling. Pastors may be less comfortable in these caregiving roles because of the complex counseling needs that are often presented. Let's pray for our pastors to sense an increased level of adequacy and empowerment with people. Our prayers are important, because only 24 percent of pastors indicate that they view meeting people's needs as a great fit with their gifts and calling.

STORIES FROM A PASTOR'S HEART

Daniel and his wife, Katherine, were confident in their ability to teach, preach, and lead the congregation, but one church member presented a particular challenge. Rachel had been a part of their congregation for the last four years. At first, Rachel's passion and enthusiasm were a breath of fresh air. Now that same fiery spirit revealed lots of anger and unforgiveness because of abuse from her past. Daniel and Katherine had counseled, exhorted, and prayed with Rachel, but nothing seemed to help.

Since David was Daniel's mentor, he offered these thoughts: "What if Rachel needs more from you? Yes, she needs to forgive, but what if she needs your comfort first?" Daniel and Katherine were good at guiding people in what to do but had no idea how to do what David suggested. Through several breakfast meetings, Daniel and Katherine learned how to give Rachel the comfort she so desperately needed. They learned to say words like, "Rachel, we're so glad that you've been able to trust us with very hard places in your life. We also want you to know that our hearts are broken for all the pain you've experienced. We're just sad because you were hurt."

Daniel and Katherine learned how to meet the need for comfort, and everyone benefitted. Rachel could begin the forgiveness process too. The congregation saw the blessing that comes when comfort is received as they witnessed Rachel's transformation.

A FRESH ENCOUNTER WITH JESUS

I created you with certain talents, gifts, and life-passions. I get great joy out of seeing you live them out. In the midst of walking out your calling, remember these two priorities: love God and love people. As you go about your day, make some time for us to spend together and then prioritize care for people. Work and ministry are my beautiful gifts, but relationships are eternal (see Ephesians 2:10; Matthew 22:36–40).

» Jesus, thank you for creating me with certain gifts and talents. I'm especially grateful for _____.

» Lord, I'm also grateful you have called some of us to teach, preach, and lead. I'm especially grateful for my pastor's gift of _____.

AN EXPERIENCE OF SCRIPTURE

We loved you so much that we shared with you not only God's Good News but our own lives, too.

—1 Thessalonians 2:8

» God, equip and empower me to not only share the good news of Jesus and live out my calling, but to share my life with the people around me.

» Help us to continue to share the gospel with many. At the same time, we pray that we would be empowered to do life with people in vulnerable and practical ways. I specifically pray my pastor would enjoy more and more of these moments.

ENGAGING GOD'S PEOPLE

Invite your pastor and spouse along with you as you have lunch with people outside the church. Give priority to building relationships.

CLAIM HIS PROMISES

The way God designed our bodies is a model for understanding our lives together as a church: every part dependent on every other part, the parts we mention and the parts we don't, the parts we see and the parts we don't. If one part hurts, every other part is involved in the hurt, and in the healing. If one part flourishes, every other part enters into the exuberance.

—1 Corinthians 12:25–26 MSG

As each one has received a special gift, employ it in serving one another as good stewards of the manifold grace of God.

—1 Peter 4:10 NASB

Love People 1:

A Spirit-empowered disciple lives a Spirit-led life of doing good in all of life: relationships, vocation, community, and calling.

Day 23

PREPARATION GAPS

Deepen our *love for people.* Equip us to shepherd others through struggles and learn to resolve conflict with courage and consistency.

*N*early three-fourths of pastors surveyed describe their training for ministry as "excellent" or "good." It appears that ministers view their formal education as making a positive impact on their preparedness for ministry. Seminary training and continuing educational opportunities obviously help close any gaps in experience or learning. We can celebrate the churches that offer continuing education for their pastors and provide opportunities for additional learning.

While we can celebrate that most pastors feel prepared by their formal educational experiences, surveys indicate two of the most common gaps in pastor preparation are knowing how to counsel people through their struggles (29 percent) and how to resolve conflict (27 percent). Because people are imperfect, the need for pastoral counseling and healing for conflicted relationships will always be important. Therefore, our prayers for pastoral wisdom and adequacy in these areas are important.

STORIES FROM A PASTOR'S HEART

At the invitation of their denominational leader, John and Caroline attended a Galatians 6:6 retreat for ministry couples. It was a chance to get away and refocus on their marriage and refuel their ministry. What the denominational leader didn't know was that John and Caroline were suffering. They were in ministry, so who could they talk to about marriage conflict? Long ago, John and Caroline had decided to coexist for the sake of the kids and their ministry. Closeness and intimacy had been replaced by coldness and regret.

This ministry couple had no idea how much God would change their perspective until they heard the facilitator ask this question: "How long has it been since you've said the words, 'I was wrong. Will you forgive me?'"

Later that evening, John and Caroline did the homework that saved their marriage and revitalized their ministry. They experienced the healing power of 1 John 1:9 as they individually talked to God about the way they had hurt their spouse and received His forgiveness. Then John shared confession with his wife. Through his tears, John described the ways he had hurt Caroline and asked for her forgiveness. Caroline vulnerably did the same. They both experienced the healing power of James 5:16 and Ephesians 4:31–32. This powerful exercise brought healing to years of unhealed hurt. The couple left the retreat with deepened marital intimacy and feeling more adequate about helping others resolve conflict.

A FRESH ENCOUNTER WITH JESUS

Conflicts are inevitable, which is why I've given you tools to heal the hurts. First, show care for one another. Demonstrating care increases unity. I love it when the people I love are in harmony. Secondly, come and let me show you any ways where you need to change. I'll be gentle, and my forgiveness is guaranteed. I want to see you grow so that you experience more and more love. Next, in humility, confess your wrongs to one another and pray for one another. Doing these brings my promise of healing (see 1 Corinthians 12:25; 1 John 1:9; James 5:16).

» Show me any hurts I need to resolve.

» Lord, please show us any confessions that need to be made. Help us resolve any conflicts with humility and grace. Empower my pastor in these same ways.

AN EXPERIENCE OF SCRIPTURE

This makes for harmony among the members, so that all the members care for each other.

—1 CORINTHIANS 12:25

» God, help me to care for others so my relationships are filled with harmony.

» Equip us with the skills, boldness, and sensitivity to resolve conflicts. I pray specifically for resolution to any conflicts our pastor may face, including _____.

ENGAGING GOD'S PEOPLE

Keep your pastor updated about your own confession and forgiveness process and with testimonies of how this has transformed your relationships at home, work, or church.

CLAIM HIS PROMISES

But if we confess our sins to him, he is faithful and just to forgive us our sins and to cleanse us from all wickedness.

—1 JOHN 1:9

Confess your sins to each other and pray for each other so that you may be healed. The earnest prayer of a righteous person has great power and produces wonderful results.

—JAMES 5:16

Love People 8:
A Spirit-empowered disciple loves people by taking courageous initiative as a peacemaker, reconciling relationships along life's journey.

Day 24

LOVING YOUR COMMUNITY

Deepen our *love for people.* Equip and empower us to teach, train, and mentor others in how to have effective, life-giving conversations.

We have much to celebrate. The majority of our pastors have a compelling vision to lead their congregations to serve others. Pastors lead their members in an average of five service projects per year, per church. These outreach initiatives allow the congregation to be the hands and feet of Jesus, to love and serve as He did. We can celebrate pastors' leadership and vision to share both the "gospel and our very life" with those outside the walls of the church (see 1 Thessalonians 2:7–8).

While we can be excited about our pastors' vision to engage the congregation in projects like food pantries, clothing drives, or neighborhood cleanup, there is still an opportunity to lift our leaders in prayer. Many, if not most, ministry leaders are insecure or uncertain how to relationally engage with the people they are serving. Only one in three pastors feel adequate to train their members in how to have effective conversations with people who are different from them.

STORIES FROM A PASTOR'S HEART

Pastor Jim felt called to lead his congregation to serve the homeless of their city, but then he realized they had a problem—he wasn't sure how to talk to the homeless community. What should he say? What conversations should be avoided? After all, he thought, "Most of the men and women who stayed at the shelter were there because of sinful choices."

Jim attended a conference where the facilitator asked an important question: "What if there could be something wrong in a person's life, and it doesn't have to do with sin?" The question shocked Jim, but he knew the answers had significant implications to ministry.

Genesis 2:18 tells us that "aloneness" was the first problem of humans. Sin didn't enter the human condition until Genesis 3. This simple but powerful truth changed things for Jim. It was the aloneness of man that brought God's first declaration of "not good." And because we have a grace-filled God, He provided for human aloneness by ordaining other relationships.

Jim was suddenly clear: "We need to focus on the aloneness of the people we serve by making friends and caring about them. We need to trust God to bring about any changes needed in their life." This clarity enabled Jim and his congregation to relax and enjoy the new opportunities to serve. Jim's congregation now effectively ministers to hundreds of homeless in their city. Lives are being changed—both inside the church and out—as God draws many people to Himself.

A FRESH ENCOUNTER WITH JESUS

I know it's hard to talk with someone who is different from you, but trust me. Trust me to empower your acceptance, en-

couragement, and comfort of others. And trust me to take care of any changes that someone else needs to make. Just concentrate on loving people like I love them. I'll take care of the rest (see Romans 15:7; 1 Thessalonians 5:11; 2 Corinthians 1:4; Romans 13:10).

» Jesus, empower me to care for others by looking for ways to give them acceptance, encouragement, comfort, or attention. I pray especially for _____.

» Lord, give us the wisdom to know how to start conversations with people who are different from us, trusting God with the rest. I pray my pastor would enjoy more moments of _____.

AN EXPERIENCE OF SCRIPTURE

… don't try to impress others. Be humble, thinking of others as better than yourselves.

—Philippians 2:3

» God, give us humility as we talk with others, especially people who are different from us. Give us questions that are motivated by care and sincere interest.

» Equip us more to talk with people who are different from us. Give us humility, insight, and motivation to learn to be friends with all kinds of different people. God, please continue to equip my pastor in _____.

ENGAGING GOD'S PEOPLE

Develop your own friendship with someone who is different from you. Encourage your pastor by sharing your story.

CLAIM HIS PROMISES

We love each other because he loved us first.

—1 JOHN 4:19

We know what real love is because Jesus gave up his life for us. So we also ought to give up our lives for our brothers and sisters.

—1 JOHN 3:16

When he comes, he will prove the world to be in the wrong about sin and righteousness and judgment.

—JOHN 16:8

Love People 4:
A Spirit-empowered disciple sees people as needing *both* redemption from sin *and* intimacy in relationships, addressing both human fallenness and aloneness.

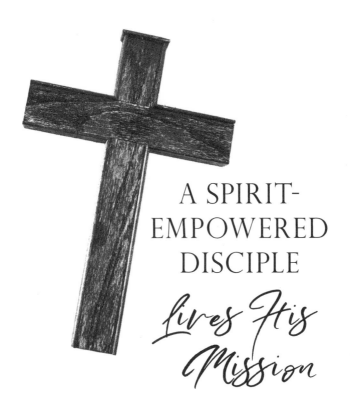

A SPIRIT-
EMPOWERED
DISCIPLE

lives His Mission

Day 25

MINISTRY PREPARATION

> Today, help us *live His mission*. Equip us in how to share life and the gospel within daily activities and relationships.

At least half (50 percent) of pastors report that their church is somewhat effective in reaching out to unchurched people and living as the hands and feet of Jesus. Almost a third of pastors viewed themselves as doing an excellent job of connecting with their neighborhood and community. We have reason to celebrate since we are each called to live out the Great Commission.

Amid positive views on connecting with the community, only one in three pastors say they feel prepared to equip their members in meaningful conversations with people outside the church. In addition, most church members feel inadequate when conversing with someone who believes differently than they do. Clearly, we have an opportunity for prayer, for growth, and for action.

STORIES FROM A PASTOR'S HEART

Pastor Brian was stumped. He had to discover how to help his congregation feel comfortable talking to their neighbors and coworkers. He was a natural extrovert and could have a conversation with any stranger, but many in his congregation weren't as comfortable. After many programs and failed attempts, Brian tried one strategy that really helped: he trained his leaders with some simple but powerful tools.

First, Brian trained his members to start a simple, celebration conversation with their coworkers or neighbors. He encouraged the congregation to ask this simple question at the beginning of a week: "What did you do this weekend?" At the end of the week, members were challenged to ask, "What fun things do you have planned for the weekend?"

Brian then taught his congregation the importance of listening for reasons to celebrate. If a neighbor mentioned attending a son's baseball game, church members were encouraged to celebrate: "Wow! That sounds fun. I know you must be proud." If a coworker talked about working in the garden over the weekend, celebrations might sound like, "That's fantastic! I'm so glad you were able to spend some time outside, doing something you enjoy." Brian and his church discovered that connecting with others on this heart level paved the way for deeper conversations about life and faith.

A FRESH ENCOUNTER WITH JESUS

I couldn't bear the thought of heaven without you, so I gave you the ultimate gift. Remember, my gift of salvation and love is new every morning. My gifts are not something in the past. I'm available every moment to help you carry life's burdens (see Lamentations 3:23; Psalm 68:19).

» Jesus, when I imagine that you couldn't bear the thought of heaven without me, I feel _____.

» Lord, when I read how your love starts over each morning and how you're available every moment to help bear my burdens, I am filled with gratitude because _____. Please give my pastor a new experience of your love today.

AN EXPERIENCE OF SCRIPTURE

Ask God to give me the right words so I can boldly explain God's mysterious plan …

—Ephesians 6:19

» God, give me the right words so I can boldly explain the mystery of God's plan to people around me. Give me boldness to tell people about the gift of your Son.

» Give us extra boldness so we can explain the mystery of God's plan in the pulpit and in daily life. Give us the right words in each relationship and opportunity. Please empower my pastor in new and specific ways _____.

ENGAGING GOD'S PEOPLE

Spend time praying the prayer above while your pastor listens. Let your pastor hear you call upon the Lord for boldness, discernment, and the right words to convey the mysterious plan of God.

CLAIM HIS PROMISES

Be strong and courageous. Do not fear or be in dread of them, for it is the Lord your God who goes with you.

—Deuteronomy 31:6 ESV

I can do all things through him who strengthens me.

—Philippians 4:13 ESV

Live His Mission 1:
A Spirit-empowered disciple loves His mission through imparting the gospel and one's very life in daily activities and relationships, vocation, and community.

Day 26

LEADING OUT
IN EVANGELISM

Help us *live His mission.* Help us to courageously and boldly lead the congregation in telling others about Jesus.

*I*n the art of evangelism, most of us have room to grow. Most pastors confirm this need when they describe their churches as being very (50 percent) or somewhat (13 percent) effective in reaching out to unchurched people. Pastors also tell us their churches have grown or remained stable in attendance over the past year. This is certainly a reason to give praise to God.

Since most church members feel inadequate to engage in meaningful conversations with unchurched friends or coworkers, pastors have an incredible opportunity to lead by example. Let's pray that our ministry leaders look for more and more opportunities to share their own stories about evangelistic conversations. We can learn a great deal from our pastors as they model listening and understanding in spiritual conversations. We will benefit from our pastors' stories of how the kindness of God's people paved the way for conviction and repentance.

STORIES FROM A PASTOR'S HEART

Pastor Ben's approach to evangelism changed this year. He realized that many in his congregation were missing some essential skills as they tried to tell their unchurched friends about Jesus. Drawn from 2 Corinthians 5:20 and our calling as Christ's ambassadors, Ben now leads what he calls "Ambassador 101" in their church.

Ben begins by equipping his church to attentively listen and vulnerably share with others. He shares his personal journey of evangelistic successes and failures to help his members deconstruct their unhelpful approaches to sharing the faith. Ben reminds his congregation to rid themselves of religious vocabulary when trying to talk to unchurched friends. He also encourages the members to let go of arguments or the goal of trying to defend God. Instead, Ben encourages the church to tell stories about how God has made a difference in their life.

Finally, Pastor Ben models his training after the conversational example of Jesus. He invites attendees to role-play, listening to one another's stories of challenge and grace. All participants practice being vulnerable with celebrations, struggles, and how Jesus is real in all of life's demands. Ben has discovered that it's the listening and vulnerability that brings closeness and commonality of shared experience. These shared experiences have paved the way for the congregation to be ready to give an account of the hope that is within them (see 1 Peter 3:15)!

A FRESH ENCOUNTER WITH JESUS

I came to seek and to save you! I didn't want to wait, so I took initiative to save you and call you to myself. I couldn't wait for you to be a part of our family. And just like the Father sent me, I am sending you. Tell people about the great things the Father has in store for those who believe. Let's celebrate our love for Him and for one another so often that you can be the first to raise your hand and say, "Here I am, Lord. Send me" (see Luke 19:10; John 20:21; Mark 16:15; Isaiah 6:8).

» Jesus, I'm grateful you didn't wait to find me. You came first to save me. I'm especially grateful because _____.

» Lord, remind us often of the initiative that you took to save us. Give us divine boldness and courage, as we seek to fulfill the Great Commission empowered by Great Commandment love. Empower my pastor to lead the congregation in this way.

AN EXPERIENCE OF SCRIPTURE

Then I heard the voice of the Lord, saying, "Whom shall I send, and who will go for Us?" And I said, "Here am I. Send me!"

—Isaiah 6:8

» God, who do you want me to talk to about your love? Here I am. Send me.

» Father, help us encourage one another in sharing our faith. May we sense a special calling to talk to specific people about you and what you are doing in our lives. Empower and encourage my pastor to lead the congregation in this way.

ENGAGING GOD'S PEOPLE

Introduce your unchurched friends to your pastor. Allow your pastor to take the lead in spiritual conversations as an encouragement and model for you to do likewise.

CLAIM HIS PROMISES

For the fruit of the righteous is a tree of life,
   and whoever captures souls is wise.

—Proverbs 11:30 ESV

For you will be a witness for him to everyone of what you have seen and heard.

—Acts 22:15 ESV

Live His Mission 8:
A Spirit-empowered disciple lives His mission through attentively listening to others' stories, vulnerably telling their story, and a sensitive sharing of Jesus' story as life's ultimate hope.

LEADING OUT IN COMMUNITY IMPACT

God, help us *live His mission*. Give us a renewed vision and initiative for ministries of compassion, love, justice, and service.

Regardless of church size, most congregations are involved in serving others outside of their church body. This commitment to community engagement is especially important since surveys of US adults indicate that most believe that churches should feed and clothe the needy, support the homeless, provide youth activities, and offer a place where people are cared for and accepted. Let's celebrate pastors as they lead their congregations into kingdom ministry outside the walls of the church.

To decrease the amount of competition for time and energy, encourage your church leadership to consider supporting existing community efforts rather than creating your own. Look for needs that are being addressed and improve upon them. Listen to congregation members as they talk about where they are already engaged in compassion and serving. Let these ideas inform church strategies to truly serve, not seeking credit for your church's own projects and programs. Millennials are especially drawn to serving for the sake of serving, so let's pray for God to multiply our efforts in community engagement.

STORIES FROM A PASTOR'S HEART

Pastor Michael listened to community leaders and church members who were local firefighters, police officers, and first responders. It was their feedback that informed the church's support for an impactful community initiative. Church and community leaders noted that a large segment of neighborhood homes lacked the protection of fire alarms. Church members realized that a city program provided fire alarms for free but distribution and installation were the challenge. Out of these opportunities and challenges, an idea was born.

The church organized themselves into multicultural teams. Some of the teams spoke Spanish, others spoke Portuguese, and a few Laotian members were represented as well. The English speakers of the church divided into groups of five or six, and Pastor Michael prepared each group for distribution. On the specified date, hundreds of home visits were made. Church members distributed and installed the free fire detection equipment for their neighbors.

As the installation concluded at each home, church members offered prayer for the residents. The prayers were unanimously received. Pastor Michael and his congregation are winning favor within their community because the church is gaining a reputation as one who serves.

A FRESH ENCOUNTER WITH JESUS

The poor and the needy are so dear to me that miraculous things happen when you give to them. Any time you meet the needs of people who are struggling, you are loving me. You honor me when you're generous to the needy. If you pour yourself out for the hungry and satisfy the needs of the afflicted, I will bring special blessings to your life. Whoever gives to the poor will not want. Remember, others will know you're my followers when they see you loving one another (see Matthew 25:40; Proverbs 14:31; 28:27; 19:17; John 13:35).

» Jesus, it's amazing that I can honor you by caring for the needs of others. I'm grateful to be able to love you in this way because _____.

» Lord, impress these truths upon our hearts in a new way. Let us love you by caring for the needs of the afflicted. Show us fresh ways to do that. Empower my pastor to love in fresh new ways as well.

AN EXPERIENCE OF SCRIPTURE

… let us not love in word or talk but in deed and in truth.

—1 JOHN 3:18 ESV

» God, show us ways to put our love into action. How can our deeds reveal your love for people?

» Jesus, give us a fresh vision for how we might love in deed and in truth. I also pray my pastor would hear from you about new ways to love.

ENGAGING GOD'S PEOPLE

Look for opportunities that are already in motion to serve your community. Join other members of your community as they serve.

CLAIM HIS PROMISES

I tell you the truth, when you did it to one of the least of these my brothers and sisters, you were doing it to me!

—MATTHEW 25:40

Whoever is generous to the poor lends to the LORD,
   and he will repay him for his deed.

—PROVERBS 19:17 ESV

If you pour yourself out for the hungry
   and satisfy the desire of the afflicted,
then shall your light rise in the darkness
   and your gloom be as the noonday.

—ISAIAH 58:10 ESV

Live His Mission 2:
A Spirit-empowered disciple lives His mission by expressing and extending the kingdom of God with compassion, justice, love, and forgiveness.

SHARING THE GOSPEL

> Allow us to *live His mission*. Let us more effectively connect with people who need to hear the gospel by living out personal interests and passions. Equip us to lead the congregation in this same strategy of reaching others for Christ.

*I*t isn't surprising that when pastors were asked to choose just one ministry task they most enjoy, two-thirds of pastors named preaching and teaching as most enjoyable. Let's celebrate that our pastors' most enjoyable task impacts the maximum amount of people through weekly worship services. Let's also celebrate that most ministry leaders are thrilled by the challenge to devote themselves to prayer and the ministry of the Word (see Acts 6:4).

While we're delighted that pastors enjoy their weekly opportunities to preach the Word, we also have an opportunity to encourage growth. When surveyed, less than 10 percent of pastors listed "sharing the gospel" as one of their most enjoyable tasks. Let's pray for passion of sharing the gospel to increase. Let's also encourage our pastors to combine weekly preaching with personal stories of their own witness with neighbors and friends. This combination of spiritual inspiration and practical example will go a long way toward equipping and encouraging members to do the same.

STORIES FROM A PASTOR'S HEART

There isn't a sport that Scott doesn't like to watch or play. Scott's love of sports has provided a great platform for building friendships with unchurched friends. Playing pickup games at the recreation center or inviting friends over to watch a ballgame has given Scott numerous opportunities to talk about his faith in Jesus.

Scott's weekly sermons include stories of how he is developing friendships that naturally lead to conversations about Jesus. Frequent baptisms of Scott's neighbors and friends provide a visual reminder to each church member that they too can be an ambassador for Christ.

While demands of a thriving ministry are significant, Scott's intentionality of becoming friends with others outside the church has provided a great example to his congregation. Church members are now turning some of their free time and outside interests into building friendships and championing Jesus.

A FRESH ENCOUNTER WITH JESUS

I've formed you with unique talents, interests, and abilities. You are my masterpiece. I created you with these gifts so that you can be a one-of-a-kind expression of me. I placed all these special abilities in you so that you can do the great things I have planned—like introduce others to me. I love to see you live out your interests and enjoy life, and I love seeing you bring my hope to this world (see Ephesians 2:10; Colossians 1:27).

» Jesus, when I imagine that you created me to be a one-of-a-kind expression of you, and you gave me these gifts to draw others to you, I feel _____.

» Lord, give us all a fresh vision for how to turn personal interests into opportunities to share Jesus. Help my pastor do this in creative ways.

AN EXPERIENCE OF SCRIPTURE

I have become all things to all people, that by all means I might save some. I do it all for the sake of the gospel, that I may share with them in its blessings.

—1 Corinthians 9:22–23 ESV

» God, show us how we can become all things to all people.

» Jesus, show us how to utilize our interests to connect with people and share the gospel. Help our pastor lead our congregation in the same way.

ENGAGING GOD'S PEOPLE

Make connections with unchurched friends around your interests. Share your story as an encouragement to your pastor.

CLAIM HIS PROMISES

For we are his workmanship, created in Christ Jesus for good works, which God prepared beforehand, that we should walk in them.

—Ephesians 2:10 ESV

And I pray that the sharing of your faith may become effective for the full knowledge of every good thing that is in us for the sake of Christ.

—Philemon 1:6 ESV

Live His Mission 3:
A Spirit-empowered disciple lives His mission by championing Jesus as the only hope of eternal life and abundant living.

NEXT-GENERATION PASSION

> Allow us to *live His mission*. Give us a fresh vision and commitment for passing on the faith to the next generation.

One in five pastors strongly agrees that their church puts a significant priority on training and developing the next generation of church leaders. Pastors exemplify this priority through personal mentoring, involving younger members in leadership roles, and establishing internships for youth, college, and young-adult leaders. As you see a commitment to developing next-generation leaders, be sure to celebrate your pastor's vision and priority.

Millennials are naturally prone to integrate their personal values and gifting in causes of justice, compassion, and the ministry of reconciliation. They desire to make a difference in their world through loving and serving others. Church leaders are wise to increase the engagement of next-generation leaders in caring, purposeful involvement outside the church.

STORIES FROM A PASTOR'S HEART

Pastor Paul found a relevant way to mentor next-generation leaders in relational evangelism. It wasn't necessarily a pretty environment, or even a pleasant-smelling one, but Paul's strategy for connecting young leaders with diverse, unchurched people was pure genius.

The first Saturday of every month, Paul would round up three or four young leaders, and they would begin "Trash Patrol." They would walk the streets of their inner-city neighborhood picking up trash and talking to anyone who would listen. Paul and his team quickly made a difference in their neglected neighborhood. As people would stop and ask, "What are you doing this for?" the Trash Patrol was able to respond, "We just care about you and our community."

Trash Patrol allowed Paul to show his next-generation leaders how to connect with people from different racial, socioeconomic, and cultural backgrounds. Their spirit of giving (with no expectations of return) broke down barriers and deepened friendships. The Trash Patrol found opportunities to share their faith with unchurched neighbors, and many were added to the kingdom because a pastor was committed to training and equipping young leaders in practical ways.

A FRESH ENCOUNTER WITH JESUS

I love to see my disciples make disciples, so entrust the wisdom, experience, and blessings you've received to other faithful disciples. Pass along the truth and the skills that you have gleaned from time with me. Physical training is of some value, but training in godliness has value for all things. Look for opportunities to mentor others. You've freely received from me, now freely give (see 2 Timothy 2:2; 1 Timothy 4:8–9; Matthew 10:8).

» Jesus, give us a clear vision for a younger brother or sister in the faith who could benefit from doing life together. Who might this person be, Lord?

» Lord, give us a renewed vision and commitment to disciple next-generation leaders. Show us who that might be and what next steps we might take to see others empowered and equipped to fulfill their calling. Give my pastor a fresh perspective on equipping younger leaders.

AN EXPERIENCE OF SCRIPTURE

Freely you have received; freely give.

—MATTHEW 10:8

» God, show me some of the wisdom, experience, or skills I have received that could be freely given to others, especially the less fortunate. How can I give to the next generation?

» Let us see our congregation from this same perspective. What have our members freely received and could now freely give to the next generation? Help our pastor lead the congregation in this way.

ENGAGING GOD'S PEOPLE

Begin developing relationships with next-generation leaders. Learn from them and look for ways you might serve the less fortunate. As an encouragement, share your experiences with your pastor.

CLAIM HIS PROMISES

If you want to be my disciple, follow me and you will go where I am going. And if you truly follow me as my disciple, the Father will shower his favor upon your life.

—JOHN 12:26 TPT

So let's not get tired of doing what is good. At just the right time we will reap a harvest of blessing if we don't give up.

—GALATIANS 6:9

Live His Mission 5:
A Spirit-empowered disciple lives His mission by ministering Christ's life and love to the "least of these."

Day 30

MAKING DISCIPLES

> Give us encouragement to *live His mission*. Renew our passion for training church members to share the gospel and for equipping disciples to make disciples.

We have reason for celebration and room to grow. Nine out of ten churches rate their discipleship or spiritual formation efforts as very (73 percent) or somewhat effective (14 percent). Ironically, most pastors and church members don't feel adequately equipped to converse with the unchurched. Therefore, look for opportunities to celebrate your pastor's example and emphasis of equipping disciples for sharing the gospel and making disciples.

Despite the sense of inadequacy that many pastors and church leaders experience, there is great opportunity to enhance the connection with unchurched friends and neighbors. Since most followers of Jesus spend much of their time engaged in work, family, and community, why not develop methods for helping church members share the gospel in these places? Training and equipping followers of Jesus to share their faith in home settings and vocational settings (integrating faith and work) will have significant kingdom impact.

STORIES FROM A PASTOR'S HEART

"Legacy Leadership" is the title of Pastor Jeff's training course. It's a resource that reveals how Jesus developed disciples as He lived life with a legacy in mind. The key objective is to equip Jesus-followers to serve others and build caring connections that enable and empower them to live out the Great Commission. Pastor Jeff has trained parents and children to apply these biblical principles as they live out their faith at home through serving and caring for one another.

Together, each family member grows in his or her role of being a person on mission. Employees and employers within the church practice the faith-at-work principles and are challenged to lead small-group discussions at their place of employment. Church members lead discussions on how to become a fully engaged employee who lives with intention and purpose. The Legacy Leadership course helps employees deliver excellence in all they do. Employers are thrilled by the results, and church leaders can impart both their life and the gospel in caring relationships throughout their place of work.

A FRESH ENCOUNTER WITH JESUS

Look for people who might need you to share your life and the gospel. Begin by taking time to be with me. One of the identifying features of my disciples is that they love to be with me. Next, be sure to share your life and the gospel with your spouse, children, family, and close friends. Then you'll want to share the good news with neighbors, coworkers, and people of your community. As you go, remember I am there with you every step of the way (see Matthew 28:19–20).

» Jesus, show us the people who need to hear about your love. With whom can we share the good news?

» Lord, give my pastor a fresh empowerment for making disciples, as well as confidence in training others.

AN EXPERIENCE OF SCRIPTURE

Come and hear, all who fear God,
And I will tell of what He has done for my soul.

—Psalm 66:16 NASB

Take a few moments to reflect on some of the recent things God has done for your soul. How has He comforted you? Saved you? Provided for you? Cared for you? Encouraged you? Guided you?

» God, thank you for _____. Now, show me a person who could benefit from hearing this story.

» Jesus, give us a new encounter with you and empowerment to tell the story of what you have done for us. Help my pastor lead the congregation in the same way.

ENGAGING GOD'S PEOPLE

Tell your Jesus story to another person. Share that experience as an encouragement to your pastor.

CLAIM HIS PROMISES

Sing to the Lord, all the earth;
Proclaim good tidings of His salvation from day to day.
Tell of His glory among the nations,
His wonderful deeds among all the peoples.
For great is the Lord, and greatly to be praised;
He also is to be feared above all gods.

—1 Chronicles 16:23–25 NASB

Live His Mission 9:
A Spirit-empowered disciple lives His mission by pouring his or her life into others, making disciples who in turn make disciples.

Day 31

CONFIDENT PEACE AND EXPECTANT FAITH

Grant us the ability to *live His mission*. Allow us to rest securely in God with confident peace and expectant faith.

*E*ven though society's moral code has been shifting away from absolute truth, and those who claim no religious preference are the fastest growing group in our nation, God always has His people. Pastors with a long view of the future resist being caught in the headlines and better navigate the complexities of our times. We can celebrate that the Holy Spirit has sustained His church for more than two thousand years, and He who began a good work will complete it (see Philippians 1:6). Look for opportunities to affirm and celebrate your pastor's confident faith in the Rock of Ages.

We are tempted to look at the craziness of our world and want things the way they used to be. That's wishful thinking. Rather than this wishful perspective, let's pray for an expectant hope and confident faith. Let's pray our pastors have the wisdom to understand the times in which we live and lead us in adapting methodologies without compromising the gospel message. The Great Commandment and the Great Commission message of loving God and living His Word, loving people, and living His mission are still relevant for our day. Let's return to a first-century priority of loving relationships that empower relevant ministry.

STORIES FROM A PASTOR'S HEART

Pastors John and Deana have a long view of ministry. It's this longevity perspective that has enabled them to pastor for more than thirty years in the same location. There was a time when this ministry couple panicked if members left the church or if demographics of the neighborhood changed. Church members who left took their tithes with them. Changing demographics often meant changing the socioeconomic profile of the congregation.

John and Deana have seen the Lord's faithfulness through rising crime rates and increased drug addiction in their small town. They've watched God abundantly provide while the average income of their congregation has lowered by 10 percent. Even though their community has been ravaged by drug addiction, John and Deana's church is known for their compassionate care and firm connection with reality. As the local school system struggled to meet the demands of vulnerable youth, John and Deana's church was approached to help to address the city's needs. As a testimony of their confidence in the Lord and as a celebration of thirty years in ministry, John and Deana's church gave thirty thousand dollars to their community's most needy!

Because John and Deana have seen God's faithfulness, they trust Him with an unwavering certainty that Great Commandment living that is empowered by Great Commandment love will stand the test of time, even in a rapidly changing world.

A FRESH ENCOUNTER WITH JESUS

One of the last promises that I gave my followers before I left the earth was this: Peace is what I leave with you. Not the world's peace, but my own peace. I know the world looks bleak at times, and I'm saddened to see the turmoil that you have had to endure.

I have overcome the world, and I hold you securely in the palm of my hand. Be strong and don't be afraid. Wait for me. I'm coming to your rescue (see John 14:27; 16:33; 1 John 5:18; Jeremiah 15:20).

» Jesus, our hope is in you. Even when we see the way the world _____, we will trust you to _____.

» Lord, remind us to take the long view of our future. Help us to see our world with an eternal perspective. Give us peace, confidence, and assurance that leads to courageous preaching and bold faith. Help my pastor see things from your perspective.

AN EXPERIENCE OF SCRIPTURE

You will keep in perfect peace
all who trust in you,
all whose thoughts are fixed on you!

—Isaiah 26:3

» God, even when we see the trouble of our lives, allow us to focus on you. We trust you to _____.

» Jesus, give us peace amid _____. Help us to focus on you, living in assurance and trust. Give my pastor an extra measure of peace because _____.

ENGAGING GOD'S PEOPLE

Ask about any worries or troubles that hinder your pastor from trusting God. Pray together, asking the Lord to keep your pastor in perfect peace.

CLAIM HIS PROMISES

The righteous will never be removed,
but the wicked will not dwell in the land.

—Proverbs 10:30 ESV

But even if you suffer for doing what is right, God will
reward you for it. So don't worry or be afraid …

—1 Peter 3:14

But all who listen to me will live in peace,
untroubled by fear of harm.

—Proverbs 1:33

Live His Mission 6:
A Spirit-empowered disciple lives His mission by demonstrating a confident peace and expectant hope in God's lordship in all things.

APPENDIX 1

ABOUT THE GREAT COMMANDMENT NETWORK

The Great Commandment Network is an international collaborative network of strategic kingdom leaders from the faith community, marketplace, education, and caregiving fields who prioritize the powerful simplicity of the words of Jesus to love God, love others, and see others become His followers (Matthew 22:37–40, Matthew 28:19–20).

THE GREAT COMMANDMENT NETWORK IS SERVED THROUGH THE FOLLOWING:

Relationship Press – This team collaborates, supports, and joins together with churches, denominational partners, and professional associates to develop, print, and produce resources that facilitate ongoing Great Commandment ministry.

The Center for Relational Leadership – Their mission is to teach, train, and mentor both ministry and corporate leaders in Great Commandment principles, seeking to equip leaders with relational skills so they might lead as Jesus led.

The Galatians 6:6 Retreat Ministry – This ministry offers a unique two-day retreat for ministers and their spouses for personal renewal and for reestablishing and affirming ministry and family priorities.

The Center for Relational Care (CRC) – The CRC provides therapy and support to relationships in crisis through an accelerated process of growth and healing, including Relational Care Intensives for couples, families, and singles.

For more information on how you, your church, ministry, denomination, or movement can be served by the Great Commandment Network write or call:

Great Commandment Network
2511 South Lakeline Blvd.
Cedar Park, Texas 78613
#800-881-8008
Or visit our website: www.GreatCommandment.net

APPENDIX 2

A SPIRIT-EMPOWERED FAITH

Expresses Itself in Great Commission Living Empowered by Great Commandment Love

 begins with the end in mind: The Great Commission calls us to make disciples.

"Go therefore and make disciples of all the nations, baptizing them in the name of the Father and the Son and the Holy Spirit teaching them to observe all things that I have commanded you; and lo, I am with you always, even to the end of the age." (Matthew 28:19–20)

The ultimate goal of our faith journey is to relate to the person of Jesus, because it is our relational connection to Jesus that will produce Christlikeness and spiritual growth. This relational perspective of discipleship is required if we hope to have a faith that is marked by the Spirit's power.

Models of discipleship that are based solely upon what we *know* and what we *do* are incomplete, lacking the empowerment of a life of loving and living intimately with Jesus. **A Spirit-empowered faith is relational and impossible to realize apart from a special work of the Spirit.** For example, the Spirit-empowered outcome of "listening to and hearing God" implies relationship—it is both relational in focus and requires the Holy Spirit's power to live.

 begins at the right place: The Great Commandment calls us to start with loving God and loving others.

"'You shall love the LORD your God with all your heart, with all your soul, and with all your mind.' This is the first and great commandment. And the second is like it: 'You shall love your neighbor as yourself.' On these two commandments hang all the Law and the Prophets."

(Matthew 22:37–40)

Relevant discipleship does not begin with doctrines or teaching, parables or stewardship—but with loving the Lord with all your heart, mind, soul, and strength and then loving the people closest to you. Since Matthew 22:37–40 gives us the first and greatest commandment, *a Spirit-empowered faith starts where the Great Commandment tells us to start: A disciple must first learn to deeply love the Lord and to express His love to the "nearest ones"—his or her family, church, and community (and in that order).*

 embraces a relational process of Christlikeness.

Scripture reminds us that there are three sources of light for our journey: Jesus, His Word, and His people. The process of discipleship (or becoming more like Jesus) occurs as we relate intimately with each source of light.

"Walk while you have the light, lest darkness overtake you." (John 12:35)

Spirit-empowered discipleship will require a lifestyle of:
* Fresh encounters with Jesus (John 8:12)
* Frequent experiences of Scripture (Psalm 119:105)
* Faithful engagement with God's people (Matthew 5:14)

 can be defined with observable outcomes using a biblical framework.

The metrics for measuring Spirit-empowered faith or the growth of a disciple come from Scripture and are organized/framed around four distinct dimensions of a disciple who serves.

And He Himself gave some to be apostles, some prophets,
some evangelists, and some pastors and teachers,
for the equipping of the saints for the work of ministry,
for the edifying of the body of Christ.
(Ephesians 4:11–12)

A relational framework for organizing Spirit-Empowered Discipleship Outcomes draws from a cluster analysis of several Greek (*diakoneo, leitourgeo, douleuo*) and Hebrew words ('*abad, Sharat*), which elaborate on the Ephesians 4:12 declaration that Christ's followers are to be equipped for works of ministry or service. Therefore, the 40 Spirit-Empowered Faith Outcomes have been identified and organized around:

- Serving/loving the Lord – *While they were **ministering** to the Lord and fasting* (Acts 13:2 NASB).[1]
- Serving/loving the Word – *But we will devote ourselves to prayer and to the **ministry** of the word* (Acts 6:4 NASB).[2]
- Serving/loving people – *Through love **serve** one another* (Galatians 5:13 NASB).[3]
- Serving/loving His mission – *Now all these things are from God, who reconciled us to Himself through Christ and gave us the **ministry** of reconciliation* (2 Corinthians 5:18 NASB).[4]

---

1 Ferguson, David L. *Great Commandment Principle*. Cedar Park, Texas: Relationship Press, 2013.

2 Ferguson, David L. *Relational Foundations*. Cedar Park, Texas: Relationship Press, 2004.

3 Ferguson, David L. *Relational Discipleship*. Cedar Park, Texas: Relationship Press, 2005.

4 "Spirit Empowered Outcomes," www.empowered21.com, Empowered 21 Global Council, http://empowered21.com/discipleship-materials/.

A SPIRIT-EMPOWERED DISCIPLE LOVES THE LORD THROUGH

L1. Practicing thanksgiving in all things
Enter into His gates with thanksgiving (Ps. 100:4). In everything give thanks (1 Th. 5:18). As sorrowful, yet always rejoicing (2 Cor. 6:10).

L2. Listening to and hearing God for direction and discernment
"Speak, LORD, for Your servant hears" (1 Sam. 3:8–9). Mary, who also sat at Jesus' feet and heard His word (Lk. 10:38–42). And the LORD said, "Shall I hide from Abraham what I am doing … ?" (Gen. 18:17). But as the same anointing teaches you concerning all things … (1 Jn. 2:27).

L3. Experiencing God as He really is through deepened intimacy with Him
"Hear, O Israel: The LORD our God, the LORD is one! You shall love the LORD your God with all your heart, with all your soul, and with all your strength" (Deut. 6:4–5). Therefore the LORD will wait, that He may be gracious to you; and therefore He will be exalted, that He may have mercy on you. For the LORD is a God of justice … (Is. 30:18). See also John 14:9.

L4. Rejoicing regularly in my identity as "His Beloved"
And his banner over me was love (Song of Sol. 2:4). To the praise of the glory of His grace, by which He made us accepted in the Beloved (Eph. 1:6). For so He gives His beloved sleep (Ps. 127:2).

L5. Living with a passionate longing for purity and to please Him in all things
Who may ascend into the hill of the LORD? … He who has clean hands and a pure heart (Ps. 24:3–4). Beloved, let us cleanse ourselves from all filthiness of flesh and spirit, perfecting holiness in the fear of God (2 Cor. 7:1). "I always do those things that please Him" (Jn. 8:29). "Though He slay me, yet will I trust Him" (Job 13:15).

L6.   Consistent practice of self-denial, fasting, and solitude rest

He turned and said to Peter, "Get behind me, Satan! You are offense to Me, for you are not mindful of the things of God, but the things of men" (Mt. 16:23). "But you, when you fast …" (Mt. 6:17). "Be still, and know that I am God" (Ps. 46:10).

L7.   Entering often into Spirit-led praise and worship

Bless the LORD, O my soul, and all that is within me (Ps. 103:1). Serve the LORD with fear (Ps. 2:11). I thank You, Father, Lord of heaven and earth (Mt. 11:25).

L8.   Disciplined, bold, and believing prayer

Praying always with all prayer and supplication in the Spirit (Eph. 6:18). "Call to Me, and I will answer you" (Jer. 33:3). If we ask anything according to His will, He hears us. And if we know that He hears us, whatever we ask, we know that we have the petitions that we have asked of Him (1 Jn. 5:14–15).

L9.   Yielding to the Spirit's fullness as life in the Spirit brings supernatural intimacy with the Lord, manifestation of divine gifts, and witness of the fruit of the Spirit

For by one Spirit we were all baptized into one body—whether Jews or Greeks, whether slaves or free—and have all been made to drink into one Spirit (1 Cor. 12:13). "But you shall receive power when the Holy Spirit has come upon you" (Acts 1:8). But the manifestation of the Spirit is given to each one for the profit of all (1 Cor. 12:7). See also 1 Pet. 4:10 and Rom. 12:6.

L10.   Practicing the presence of the Lord, yielding to the Spirit's work of Christlikeness

But we all, with unveiled face, … are being transformed into the same from glory to glory, just as by the Spirit of the Lord (2 Cor. 3:18). As the deer pants for the water brooks, so pants my soul after You, O God (Ps. 42:1).

A SPIRIT-EMPOWERED DISCIPLE LIVES THE WORD THROUGH

W1. Frequently being led by the Spirit into deeper love for the One who wrote the Word

" 'You shall love the Lord your God … .' 'You shall love neighbor as yourself.' On these two commandments hang all the Law and the Prophets" (Mt. 22:37–40). And I will delight myself in Your commandments, which I love. (Ps. 119:47). "The fear of the LORD is clean … . More to be desired are they than gold … sweeter also than honey" (Ps. 19:9–10).

W2. Being a "living epistle" in reverence and awe as His Word becomes real in my life, vocation, and calling

You are our epistle written in our hearts, known and read by all men (2 Cor. 3:2). And the Word became flesh and dwelt among us (Jn. 1:14). Husbands, love your wives … cleanse her with the washing of water by the word (Eph. 5:25–26). See also Tit. 2:5. And whatever you do, do it heartily, as to the Lord and not to men (Col. 3:23).

W3. Yielding to the Scripture's protective cautions and transforming power to bring life change in me

Through Your precepts I get understanding; therefore I hate every false way (Ps. 119:104). "Let it be to me according to your word" (Lk. 1:38). How can a young man cleanse his way? By taking heed according to Your word (Ps. 119:9). See also Col. 3:16–17.

W4. Humbly and vulnerably sharing of the Spirit's transforming work through the Word

I will speak of your testimonies also before kings, and will not be ashamed (Ps. 119:46). Preach the word! Be ready in season and out of season (2 Tim. 4:2).

W5. Meditating consistently on more and more of the Word hidden in the heart

Your word I have hidden in my heart, that I might not sin against You (Ps. 119:11). *Let the words of my mouth and the meditation of my heart be acceptable in Your sight, O Lord, my strength and my Redeemer* (Ps. 19:14).

W6. Encountering Jesus in the Word for deepened transformation in Christlikeness

But we all, with unveiled face, … are being transformed into the same image from glory to glory, just as by the Spirit of the Lord (2 Cor. 3:18). *If you abide in Me, and My words abide in you, you will ask what you desire, and it shall be done for you* (Jn. 15:7). See also Lk. 24:32, Ps. 119:136, and 2 Cor. 1:20.

W7. A life explained as one of "experiencing Scripture"

But this is what was spoken by the prophet Joel (Acts 2:16). *This is my comfort in my affliction, for Your word has given me life* (Ps. 119:50). *My soul breaks with longing for Your judgements at all times* (Ps. 119:20).

W8. Living "naturally supernatural" in all of life as His Spirit makes the written Word (*logos*) the living Word (*rhema*)

*So then aith comes by hearing, and hearing by the word (*rhema*) of God* (Rom. 10:17). *Your word is a lamp to my feet and a light to my path* (Ps. 119:105).

W9. Living abundantly "in the present" as His Word brings healing to hurt and anger, guilt, fear, and condemnation—which are heart hindrances to life abundant

"The thief does not come except to steal, and to kill, and to destroy" (Jn. 10:10). *I will run the course of Your commandments, for You shall enlarge my heart* (Ps. 119:32). *"And you shall know the truth, and the truth shall make you free"* (Jn. 8:32). *Stand fast therefore in the liberty by which Christ has made us free, and do not be entangled again with a yoke of bondage* (Gal. 5:1).

W10. Implicit, unwavering trust that His Word will never fail
"The grass withers, the flower fades, but the word of our God stands forever"
(Is. 40:8). *"So shall My word be that goes forth from My mouth; it shall not return
to Me void"* (Is. 55:11).

A SPIRIT-EMPOWERED DISCIPLE LOVES PEOPLE THROUGH

**P1. Living a Spirit-led life of doing good in all of life: relationships and
vocation, community and calling**
Who went about doing good … (Acts 10:38). *"Let your light so shine before men,
that they may see your good works and glorify your Father in heaven"* (Mt. 5:16).
*"But love your enemies, do good, and lend, hoping for nothing in return; and your
reward will be great, and you will be sons of the Most High. For He is kind to the
unthankful and evil"* (Lk. 6:35). See also Rom. 15:2.

P2. "Startling people" with loving initiatives to "give first"
*"Give, and it will be given to you: good measure, pressed down, shaken together,
and running over will be put into your bosom"* (Lk. 6:38). *Then Jesus said, "Father,
forgive them, for they do not know what they do"* (Lk. 23:34). See also Lk. 23:43
and Jn. 19:27.

P3. Discerning the relational needs of others with a heart to give of His love
*Let no corrupt word proceed out of your mouth, but what is good for necessary
edification, that it might impart grace to the hearers* (Eph. 4:29). *And my God
shall supply all your need according to His riches in glory by Christ Jesus* (Phil.
4:19). See also Lk. 6:30.

P4.   Seeing people as needing BOTH redemption from sin AND intimacy in relationships, addressing both human fallen-ness and aloneness

But God demonstrates His own love toward us, in that while we were still sinners, Christ died for us (Rom. 5:8). *And when Jesus came to the place, He looked up and saw him, and said to him, "Zacchaeus, make haste and come down, for today I must stay at your house"* (Lk. 19:5). See also Mk. 8:24 and Gen. 2:18.

P5.   Ministering His life and love to our nearest ones at home and with family as well as faithful engagement in His body, the church

Husbands, likewise, dwell with them with understanding, giving honor to the wife, as to the weaker vessel, and as being heirs together of the grace of life, that your prayers may not be hindered (1 Pet. 3:7). See also 1 Pet. 3:1 and Ps. 127:3.

P6.   Expressing the fruit of the Spirit as a lifestyle and identity

But the fruit of the Spirit is love, joy, peace, longsuffering, kindness, goodness, faithfulness, gentleness, self-control (Gal. 5:22–23). *A man's stomach shall be satisfied from the fruit of his mouth; From the produce of his lips he shall be filled* (Prov. 18:20).

P7.   Expecting and demonstrating the supernatural as His spiritual gifts are made manifest and His grace is at work by His Spirit

In mighty signs and wonders, by the power of the Spirit of God, so that from Jerusalem and round about to Illyricum I have fully preached the gospel of Christ (Rom. 15:19). *"Most assuredly, I say to you, he who believes in Me, the works that I do he will do also"* (Jn. 14:12). See also 1 Cor. 14:1.

P8.   Taking courageous initiative as a peacemaker, reconciling relationships along life's journey

Be at peace among yourselves (1 Th. 5:13). *For He Himself is our peace, who has made both one, and has broken down the middle wall of separation* (Eph. 2:14). *Confess your trespasses to one another, and pray for one another, that you may be healed* (Jas. 5:16).

P9. Demonstrating His love to an ever growing network of "others" as He continues to challenge us to love "beyond our comfort"

He who says, "I know Him," and does not keep His commandments, is a liar, and the truth is not in him (1 Jn. 2:4). If someone says, "I love God," and hates his brother, he is a liar; for he who does not love his brother whom he has seen, how can he love God whom he has not seen? (1 Jn. 4:20).

P10. Humbly acknowledging to the Lord, ourselves, and others that it is Jesus in and through us who is loving others at their point of need

"Take My yoke upon you and learn from Me, for I am gentle and lowly in heart, and you will find rest for your souls" (Mt. 11:29). "If I then, your Lord and Teacher, have washed your feet, you also ought to wash one another's feet" (Jn. 13:14).

A SPIRIT-EMPOWERED DISCIPLE LIVES HIS MISSION THROUGH

M1. Imparting the gospel and one's very life in daily activities and relationships, vocation and community

So, affectionately longing for you, we were well pleased to impart to you not only the gospel of God, but also our own lives, because you had become dear to us (1 Th. 2:8–9). See also Eph. 6:19.

M2. Expressing and extending the kingdom of God as compassion, justice, love, and forgiveness are shared

"I must preach the kingdom of God to the other cities also, because for this purpose I have been sent" (Lk. 4:43). "As You sent Me into the world, I also have sent them into the world" (Jn. 17:18). Restore to me the joy of Your salvation, and uphold me by Your generous Spirit. Then I will teach transgressors Your ways, and sinners shall be converted to You (Ps. 51:12–13). See also Mic. 6:8.

M3. Championing Jesus as the only hope of eternal life and abundant living

"Nor is there salvation in any other, for there is no other name under heaven given among men by which we must be saved" (Acts 4:12). *"The thief does not come except to steal, and to kill, and to destroy. I have come so that they may have life, and that they have it more abundantly"* (Jn. 10:10). See also Acts 4:12 and Jn. 14:6.

M4. Yielding to the Spirit's role to convict others as He chooses, resisting expressions of condemnation

"And when He has come, He will convict the world of sin, and of righteousness, and of judgment" (Jn. 16:8). *Who is he who condemns? It is Christ who died, and furthermore is also risen, who is even at the right hand of God, who also makes intercession for us* (Rom. 8:34). See also Rom. 8:1.

M5. Ministering His life and love to the "least of these"

"Then He will answer them saying, 'Assuredly, I say to you inasmuch as you did not do it to one of the least of these, you did not do it to Me' " (Mt. 25:45). *Pure and undefiled religion before God and the Father is this: to visit orphans and widows in their trouble, and to keep oneself unspotted from the world* (Jas. 1:27).

M6.   Bearing witness of a confident peace and expectant hope in God's lordship in all things

Now may the Lord of peace Himself give you peace always in every way. The Lord be with you all (2 Thess. 3:16). *And let the peace of God rule in your hearts, to which also you were called in one body; and be thankful* (Col. 3:15). See also Rom. 8:28 and Ps. 146:5.

M7.   Faithfully sharing of time, talent, gifts, and resources in furthering His mission

Of which I became a minister according to the stewardship from God which was given to me for you, to fulfill the word of God (Col. 1:25). *"For everyone to whom much is given, from him much will be required"* (Lk. 12:48). See also 1 Cor. 4:1–2.

M8.   Attentive listening to others' story, vulnerably sharing of our story, and a sensitive witness of Jesus' story as life's ultimate hope; developing your story of prodigal, preoccupied and pain-filled living; listening for others' story and sharing Jesus' story

But sanctify the Lord God in your hearts, and always be ready to give a defense to everyone who asks you a reason for the hope that is in you, with meekness and fear (1 Pet. 3:15). *"For this my son was dead and is alive again"* (Luke 15:24). See also Mk. 5:21–42 and Jn. 9:1–35.

M9.   Pouring our life into others, making disciples who in turn make disciples of others

"Go therefore and make disciples of all the nations, baptizing them in the name of the Father and of the Son and of the Holy Spirit, teaching them to observe all things that I commanded you; and lo, I am with you always, even to the end of the age" (Mt. 28:19–20). See also 2 Tim. 2:2.

M10. Living submissively within His body, the Church, as instruction and encouragement; reproof and correction are graciously received by faithful disciples

Submitting to one another in the fear of God (Eph. 5:21). *Brethren, if a man is overtaken in any trespass, you who are spiritual restore such a one in a spirit of gentleness, considering yourself lest you also be tempted* (Gal. 6:1). See also Gal. 6:2.

How Are Spiritual Leaders Doing Today?

In the not-too-distant past, a career in church ministry might have appealed to any leader who sought recognition and respect. Today, however, Christian ministers are as likely to be ignored by the broader culture as they are to be admired.

Despite daunting challenges, called and committed pastors are essential to lead God's people. The shrinking, increasingly marginalized Christian community needs wise, humble shepherds to guide them through the wilderness ahead. So how are these leaders doing?

The State of Pastors contains the findings of a comprehensive, whole-life assessment of US pastors, commissioned by Pepperdine University. The research examines church leaders' perceptions of:

- Their own mental, physical, financial, emotional and spiritual well-being
- The health of their relationships with family and church members
- Their ministry's overall health and effectiveness
- How they are received as a leader by their local community
- Their support system, including mentors, friends and fellow ministers
- How well their skills, gifts and calling align with their pastoral responsibilities
- And much more

The challenges of pastoring in the twenty-first century are significant. Yet based on these findings, Barna researchers believe many of today's pastors are prepared to be adaptive leaders: ready to be changed by the Spirit in order to bring the unchanging gospel to people in need of good news. *The State of Pastors* reveals where church leaders are most in need of healing and encouragement, and offers hopeful counsel for pastors (and those who love them). To purchase this resource, go to barna.com.